maturing as Ambassadors of Jesus

A Trilogy - Part 2

maturing as AMBASSADORS of *JESUS*

lessons from my life

MARION "MIKE" MENNING
an autobiography

Praise for *Maturing as Ambassadors of Jesus*

"When one serves in the kingdom as long as Mike Menning; when that person perseveres through hardships, there grows a sweet humility and submission to Christ that makes God look amazing. Through his tireless labors, my friend Mike has come to view challenges as his allies. In short, hardship has made Mike Menning a man of solid character, and it is why *Becoming Ambassadors of Jesus* and *Maturing Ambassadors of Jesus* are worthy reading. Like any believer who has Christ's interests at heart, Mike cannot keep God's blessings to himself. He is heaven-bent on passing his hard-won wisdom to others. Through his amazing story, you will learn that there is a suffering Savior to cleave to, a kingdom to forcefully advance, and a God in heaven to honor through every hardship. It's what you'll discover by reading these books!"

—Joni Eareckson Tada, President and Founder of Joni and
Friends International Disability Center - Woodland Hills, CA

"If you love a thumping good story, Mike Menning's books are for you. You will be enthralled as Mike tells you the stories that have shaped his life. Beyond great storytelling, Mike's book will bolster and ignite your faith as he testifies to the power and grace of the risen Christ. You will be captivated, stirred and deeply encouraged by *Becoming Ambassadors of Jesus* and *Maturing Ambassadors of Jesus* as you consider how you, too, can be an envoy for Jesus in every aspect of your life."

—Lorilee Craker, *New York Times* bestselling author of
15 books, including, *My Journey to Heaven* with Marv Besteman
- Grand Rapids, MI

"I have known Mike for almost two decades. I know him to be a man committed to the growth and development of God's people. This work is an example of his heart to reach the family of Christ with a message and stories that will shape the life of any believer. This book is perfectly matched for our time. After reading this work, I am confident that it is a worthy tool for personal Christian growth, small group curriculum, or a church-wide sermon series. Thank you Mike for pouring your heart into this project, and for sharing the most intimate stories of your life journey. We are all the better for it!"

—Corey J. Hodges, Pastor of The Point Church,
Chaplin for the NBA Utah Jazz - Salt Lake City, UT

"Some seek a destination and then travel the path their own way. Others seek to discover and follow the path set before them. Mike's story is certainly about what happens along that path set by God. His testimony is the obedience lived following the path of the God he serves. Be inspired. Proverbs 3:6."

—David VanNingen, Retired CEO of Hope Haven,
Inc. and Hope Haven International - Rock Valley, IA

"I have had a 50-year God-blessed friendship with Mike and Dawn Menning. I know his love for Christ and family and countless others. I know his amazing determination to do the right thing and humility to repent of the wrong thing. You will surely receive a blessing from reading *Becoming Ambassadors of Jesus* and *Maturing Ambassadors of Jesus*. The life lessons of sorrows, setbacks, and suffering, and ultimate victories in and through Christ will be of great encouragement to you."

—Glen Sherwood, Ph.D., Former Minnesota State Representative,
Minority Leader, Pastor, and Church Planter - Hermosa, SD

"Mike's *modus operandi* (MO) is what I have gleaned so much from my decades of contact with Mike Menning. Mike's MO (*modus operandi*) is what helps other people mature. That MO is marked by this: Mike knows that doing things for other people in an attempt to make them become better Christians, does not work. It makes people dependent and even lazy in their faith and practice. In my friendship with Mike, I have seen him operate with the understanding that people must take responsibility for their own development in life. He will encourage, and give guidance, but will allow the other person to own his/her own actions and life. Read *Becoming Ambassadors of Jesus* and *Maturing Ambassadors of Jesus* and see this principle at work."

—Pastor Gilbert Kamps, Christian Reformed Church
- Manhattan, MT

"If you want to understand how to walk in the steps of Jesus, Mike Menning's stories will inspire you to take steps of faith you never thought you could. Mike has been a friend and mentor to me, an example of what it means to be a bold leader. Mike is an Ambassador of Jesus, a fighter against injustice, compassionate to those struggling, and a constant witness of Jesus' power to save and heal. His life is an example for all Christians. He serves with humility, sacrifice, kindness, strength, and a never-ending commitment to the gospel despite many personal trials and tribulations. The thing I admire most about Mike is that even though he tirelessly works to overcome injustice, he always has time for individuals, whether they be governors or the downtrodden. I hope you get as much enjoyment out of Mike's stories as I have. And I hope you will reflect on your own life and be inspired to take greater steps of faith in obedience to our Lord Jesus Christ."

—Dave Elshaug, Director of Loving Utah
- South Jordan, UT

"*Becoming Ambassadors of Jesus* and *Maturing Ambassadors of Jesus* are the right titles for this amazing testimony. Mike Menning, always the engaging storyteller, shares chapter after chapter on how God weaves together seemingly impossible or random circumstances to achieve God's Kingdom purposes. As a co-laborer with Mike on part of his journey, I can testify that lives were changed beyond our expectations through Mike's humble insistence to follow where God led. An inspiring read!"

—Andrew Ryskamp, Director-Emeritus, World Renew
- Grand Rapids, MI

"I love people's stories. I love how Jesus is the author of our stories, and I love Mike Menning. Mike is one of the most faithful servants of Jesus I know. I am one of many who have been the recipient of Mike's never-ending encouragement to stay the course and trust in God. In *Becoming Ambassadors of Jesus* and *Maturing Ambassadors of Jesus*, you get to join Mike in his journey through life. His story reveals how Mike became the godly man he is. He found God to be faithful, put his trust in Him, and through His grace, God has made Mike faithful. If you could use some encouragement to keep going strong in your faith and to believe in God for great things, I'd encourage you to read these books. And if the opportunity arises, grab a coffee with Mike!"

— Dave Nelson, Lead Pastor, K2 the Church
- Salt Lake City, UT

"This is not just a memoir of an intriguing and compelling man, it is an investment guide. *Becoming Ambassadors of Jesus* and *Maturing Ambassadors of Jesus* are the story of a man who "walked life" with a variety of people and encouraged them to make much of this life by investing it for eternity. I speak from experience! Mike's mentorship proved invaluable as we journeyed into the mysterious interior of the FLDS communities of southern Utah and northern Arizona. God used Mike as a compassionate soldier fighting for the good of the oppressed and the spiritually malnourished. He was guided by his commitment to the gospel of Jesus and his passion for their eternal souls. These books are a perfect companion for those who wish to invest well by investing in people."

—Brody Olson, Church Planter in Polygamist Community of Hildale, UT/Colorado City, AZ - Hildale, UT

"*Becoming Ambassadors of Jesus* and *Maturing Ambassadors of Jesus* chronicle how our sovereign God in His grace empowers an ordinary man to do momentous things for the kingdom. The compelling character of these books is that page after page the reader is cajoled and challenged to be as open to God's plan and power as Mike Menning."

—Rev. Jack Gray, Pastor Emeritus, Christian Reformed Church - Sioux Falls, SD

"*Becoming Ambassadors of Jesus* and *Maturing Ambassadors of Jesus* are stories of a life well-lived, lived, that is, to glorify God. Mike and I met in the late 1970s. Immediately I saw the evidence that this was a man of convictions. I saw a man committed to faith in Christ, love of family, and dedicated to public policy. Mike Menning was and is the real thing. Mike's office became a gathering place for pro-life, pro-family, and pro-decency leaders. His highest priority, however, was to share the Good News of the Gospel of Jesus Christ. I know Mike Menning as the man who introduced me to principle-driven politics, self-improvement, standing tall amid immense pressure publicly, and meeting the challenges of private and family life. I watched as Mike moved from the mission field at the Legislature to a series of mission fields, still calling people to faith in Christ. I believe he will continue to do so until God calls him home."

—Dave Racer, MLitt, Writer, Researcher, Teacher, Publisher - Woodbury, MN

I dedicate this book, *Maturing as Ambassadors of Jesus*, to my Lord and Savior, Jesus Christ. All praise for my life and the need to share the stories are not of my doing, but it was the Lord who laid on my heart the writing of this book.

Contents

Section Five - God's Humor, Angels, and Ambassadorship

Section Six - Life Beyond Imagination

Foreword

By Dawn Menning

For now, I will try to write a "foreword" - a short introduction to this book, *Maturing as Ambassadors of Jesus*. However, when I consider the word "foreword" and the life I have shared with my husband, it leads me to the word, "forward." For over sixty years, he and I have walked life together; each moment, day, month, and year has been a forward movement, even amidst setbacks, valleys, and redo moments as well.

In the summer of 1962, I was a young farm girl loving life, enjoying high school and all the activities and extracurriculars I could manage to fit into my schedule. Then along came a guy who seemed interested in me. In Book 1, he tells the hilarious effort he made to ask me for our first date!

Fast forward to June 14, 1968. On that day, I assumed a new title and became Dawn Menning. After our wedding, as we were leaving our hometown, Marion surprised me by mentioning there was one thing he wished to pursue in the coming years – to dabble with local politics. I remember thinking, "Whatever!" I was more interested in thinking of our new lives together.

Such were the surprises that followed. I saw my boyfriend climb some pretty high mountains by then and in the coming years I saw my husband pursuing and overcoming things I hadn't dreamed would be possible. He and I scrambled over some high peaks and navigated some deep waters. However, each time there was one thing that never left us - hope and a forward vision. We hoped for God's best for us and later for our sons.

Many years ago I was asked to share my life story and I claimed my life verse, Proverbs 3:5-6. "Trust in the LORD with all your heart and lean not on your own understanding; in all your ways submit to him and he will make your paths straight." [NIV] I knew the first part was true because that's what I did - trust the Lord. I also knew I didn't understand a lot about my life! I prayed often to submit to Jesus and then I got to the part about straight paths. Oh my. We had no such thing as straight paths in our lives! I never dreamed our lives could take so many turns, and even twists, to be on God's path. But when I look back I see clearly that each path was part of the journey of our lives, not only mine and Marion's, but also our sons and later our son, Mitchell's life with his wife, Kara, and their six children. That alone could fill another book!

More recently, on November 9, Mike and I read our morning devotion together from a book by Joni Eareckson Tada. This month she is leading us on a journey of considering the purpose of suffering. That day she pointed us to a time for everything, Ecclesiastes 3:1. "There's an opportune time to do things, a right time for everything on the earth." [MSG] Regarding this, Joni comments, "That's because God's answers and purposes have to be *lived out* to understand them. And that takes time and trust."[1]

On that day, I realized I don't *understand* much about our lives or even the *purposes* of much in my life, including the writing of these books by Mike. However, the words *time and trust* mean much to me!

It's not about my time; that's up to God. But it is about my TRUST. God is trustworthy and faithful and I have been called to trust and be faithful in life, with Mike, Michael, the rest of our family, and God's entire family here on earth.

This trust allows me to look forward to what He has in store for us in eternity, as together we mature as Ambassadors of Jesus.

Dawn Menning
Wife of Marion "Mike" Menning

Introduction

Therefore, we are ambassadors for Christ,
God making his appeal through us.
2 Corinthians 5:20a [ESV]

So even to old age and gray hairs, O God, do not forsake me,
until I proclaim your might to another
generation, your power to all those to come.
Psalm 71:18 [ESV]

My prayer is that as you read my autobiography you will not so much remember Mike Menning, my stories, and my life, but that you will recognize God's faithfulness in YOUR life, examine your call to ambassadorship, and trust Him more, and more.

Some have asked, "Why at your age, would you go through the daunting task of writing not only one book, but a trilogy on ambassadorship - there are many other things to do in one's retirement, right?" The short answer is that I need to be obedient to God's guidance.

As I grew older, I felt God nudging me to give a new Bible to our son Mitch, his wife Kara, each of our grandkids, Isaiah, Joey, Ellie, Cyndi, Luther, Asher, and a few other special people in our lives. I wanted to go through each of these Bibles chronologically, date each chapter as I read it, and write personal applications and notes to each one. I soon realized that doing this with about a dozen Bibles would take me a considerable amount of time.

Early every morning for three years I sat down with a cup of coffee, my AirPods in place, and my pen in my hand. I placed that morning's date at the beginning of every chapter that I read. I felt led to underline certain verses and phrases and make notes to my recipients as God led me through the process. Each morning, six days a week I finished somewhere between eight and sometimes as many as twelve chapters. In this process, I received blessings beyond my wildest dreams. One of those blessings was that as I read the Bible chronologically, certain themes that I had not discovered in the past seemed to jump off the pages of scripture. One of those themes was that we must not only tell and retell the old story of the great gifts of salvation and God's love, but we must tell future generations of God's powerful working and faithfulness in our lives. It's not just a suggestion – it's a command.

At the same time that I was doing this, I began writing my autobiography. I thought I knew how much work was ahead because of my experience with my first book, *Us Four: A Senator, His Family, Their Brain Injured Child.* I knew I had to discipline myself and carry through with the work. It all started with showing how God took us through life's mountain peaks and deep valleys.

About a third of the way into the manuscript God laid on my heart the need to complete the project because what I was doing was important work. I realized I needed to make the book available to the public and that it could be used for small group Bible study, or as I like to say, encouragement for putting God's Word into action.

The Bible teaches that all believers should be ambassadors of Jesus. I took this teaching seriously and realized more and more that the first part of my life's journey was God leading me to "become" an ambassador of Jesus. Part Two of the trilogy, *Maturing as An Ambassador of Jesus* deals with God helping me on my journey. Part Three of the trilogy will be the story of our son Michael, his disability, and his ambassadorship. In that book, I will challenge the church about how to respond to people with disabilities, all based on Matthew 11:4. Finally, I will bring to light unsung heroes of people and churches who are making a difference in the lives of ALL God's family.

I pray that as you read this book you reflect on and ponder your own life; and that you grow closer and closer to our Lord and Savior, Jesus Christ.

In His service,
Marion "Mike" Menning

Before You Begin Reading...

Please ask yourself the following questions

*So we are Christ's **ambassadors**; God is making his **appeal**
through us. We speak for Christ when we plead,
"Come back to God."*
2 Corinthians 5:20 [NLT]

Reflect on your life concerning the words from the above verse:

What does the word **ambassadors** mean to you?

What does the word **appeal** mean to you?

What does **through us** mean to you?

Pondering your life's direction

Be encouraged to ponder what an Ambassador of Jesus looks
like as you read the second half of Mike's story.

Section One

Changes, Governor's Race, Full-Time Ministry

One

Big Changes and Confirmation

*Peace I leave with you; my peace I give you. I do not give to you
as the world gives. Do not let your hearts be troubled
and do not be afraid.*

John 14:27 [NIV]

Within a matter of a few months, our family was going through incredible and dynamic changes. For four and half years our youngest son, Michael, by now age seven, had been in many ways the center of our universe. We worked on his home-based brain stimulation program ten hours a day, seven days a week, sometimes involving over ten volunteers coming into our home every day. Two hundred great people who believed in Michael and what we were doing came from near and far. This program was administered by The Institutes for the Achievement of Human Potential based in Philadelphia, Pennsylvania. It was designed to help Michael's brain further develop and was incredibly successful. But after four and half years his progress had plateaued. We were exhausted and decided that the program was no longer helping him.

The superintendent of the Edgerton Public Schools, Bill Richter, came to inform us that Michael needed to be enrolled and begin his formal education. He was a good man, he not only informed us of

1

the federal law concerning the need for all children to be in a school program, but he ministered to us as hurting parents of a child with severe disabilities. Under the law ultimately the school district was responsible for ensuring that all children receive a formal education. The problem was that in the mid-1980s the Edgerton Minnesota Public School District was unable to meet Michael's needs.

It seemed like the best we could do was to place Michael in a highly specialized boarding school called Institutes of Logopedics, Wichita, Kansas. We enrolled Michael. The pain in our hearts over the thoughts of separation from our son living in Wichita was indescribable.

I cannot imagine the pain Michael felt missing us, when he was in Wichita and was unable to communicate because he could not speak. Our oldest son Mitch, two years older than Michael, hadn't known what life was like without his little brain-injured brother; he too seemed lost. It was a fact that for the past four and half years my wife Dawn had worked 60 to 70 hours a week with Michael's program. I was very concerned for her, she also was going through extremely hard times. Yes, our lives had revolved around working with Michael.

For a couple of months, I was also like a fish out of water. I was 38 years old, had been a three-term state legislator, and then found myself facing gigantic family challenges. We were all trying to adjust to some normalcy outside of public life.

Six weeks after we left Michael at the Institutes in Wichita, the superintendent of our schools told us that the Federal Title 19 program would not pay the tuition at the Institutes and that Michael had to return home until something else could be worked out. Not only that, our insurance payment was going to stop! We were confused, but deep down we were jumping for joy, Michael was coming home! In working with the school an agreement was reached. We enrolled Michael in a wonderful, specialized boarding school in Sioux Falls, South Dakota – an hour's drive from our home. Michael stayed at school during the week.

With Mitchell and Michael in school, Dawn was able to use her gifts as a special assistant to the director of a nearby Christian alcohol and drug treatment center, New Life Treatment Center, in Woodstock, Minnesota.

I went full-speed into the management and operation of our new company, Menning Energy Systems. However, after two years I felt led to get back into Minnesota's big picture. Buyers for our newly established corporation came along, and as the old saying goes, "Sold lock, stock, and barrel."

Minnesota's business climate was in horrible shape at the time with extremely high state corporate taxes. The cost of workers and unemployment compensation were going through the ceiling. Over several years Minnesota had lost 85,000 jobs to neighboring states. I saw an opportunity to take some action.

I organized key business people from around the state and together we formed an organization called Minnesota Proposition 180. Our goal was to turn Minnesota's business and job climate around 180 degrees. I hired David Racer, a good friend, to be my Executive Director. Our headquarters were in St. Paul, Minnesota. Dave took care of a lot of the details. He set speaking engagements for me. I was the front guy, the spokesman.

1984 was very busy for me. My new work and challenge was to bring the message to voters. I spoke at Kiwanis Clubs, Rotary Clubs, Chamber of Commerce meetings, and any other groups that would have me. I spoke at many Republican rallies as well. We made media appearances before and after my speeches. That year I drove over 40,000 miles and gave over 300 speeches. I wrote the blueprint for the campaigns of twenty-four Republican candidates running for the legislature. The major media in the Twin Cities and most small-town newspapers, radio, and television carried the message of what we were doing. Some even finished their stories with comments like, "There is no doubt if Menning pulls this off he will be the Republican's favorite for governor two years from now." That idea intrigued me and got me thinking.

On election day of 1984, I joined my friends in the Twin Cities and awaited the results. Many of our candidates won, and it was enough to place the Republicans in control of the State House. Many media outlets called asking me when I planned to announce my race for Governor of Minnesota.

I went home and took time to regroup. I felt God working in my heart to do just that - run for Governor of Minnesota. At first, Dawn was not so sure. We had many discussions, including how a state-wide campaign would affect our family and how we as a family would handle the fact that I would be campaigning for nearly two years. There was also the consideration that if I won, life would be very different living in the Governor's Mansion. We would have full-time security, not only for me but for Dawn and the boys as well.

I spent much time talking to the Lord about this big decision. I spent time in God's Word and sought the advice of several Godly people. Just as in other times, once again the Lord led me to John 14:27, "Peace I leave with you; my peace I give you. I do not give to you as the world gives. Do not let your hearts be troubled and do not be afraid." [NIV] My prayer was that if God did not give me peace to run, I would not run, and if He gave me peace, I would know God was leading me to announce my candidacy for governor.

Encouragement to run for governor came from many parts of the state. Dawn agreed, although somewhat reluctantly at first. She became very supportive and worked hard traveling the state on my behalf.

In February 1985, we established the Menning for Governor Exploratory Committee and opened an office in St. Paul. Once again my good friend Dave Racer was at my side as my first campaign manager. We were off to a running start.

For the first couple of weeks, Dave and I were jam-packed with organizing, planning, renting an office, and gathering used office furniture and equipment. For me, it was fundraising, fundraising, and more fundraising. My personal space and home away from home was a room downstairs in Dave's parent's home. They offered the apartment rent-free to me which certainly helped in cutting costs while I stayed in the Twin Cities.

Since I was seeking the Republican nomination for governor, my goal was to get my message out to the public and to the Republican activists, all at the same time. I had to raise money and speak at every Republican gathering across the state that I could get to, and at any public venue I could catch.

Most of the time, I left home very early on Monday mornings and returned on Saturday nights. At first, I hired a young man from Worthington to be my assistant and driver. Later, Curt De Kam, a single young man from Edgerton, was hired to fill that position. He was with me 24/6, as he and I were usually home on Sunday. As we traveled, crisscrossing the state, I often slept in the back seat of my car and many times in small airplanes. At that time while in the Twin Cities, we were invited to move into the home of Curly Hawkins, a longtime Christian brother, and chair of our finance committee. This allowed both Curt and me to be comfortable when we were not on the road.

I was the first to announce my race for the Republican nomination for Minnesota Governor. At the peak of the campaign, thirteen candidates were running for the Republican nomination for that position. Some announced, ran, and after six or seven months most dropped out of the race.

Running for Governor was one of the most challenging things I had ever done. On a good night, I got to sleep in a bed for more than six hours.

God blessed me with great health. I was able to continue to raise money. Dave Racer, my first campaign manager, made the appointments with the heavy hitters and I had to face them eyeball to eyeball and ask for the money, this system worked well.

At the peak of our campaign, my name recognition was 74% throughout the entire state of Minnesota. One of the major newspapers published an article saying that as far as the endorsement was concerned, it was all over but the shouting. They said that I was going to "walk off" with the nomination, but I found that hard to believe. That said, the staff and I always worked as if we needed to do just a little more before the endorsing convention.

One of the campaign policies I insisted on was that we would **not borrow** money. If the money wasn't there, we simply didn't spend more than we had. If the money stopped coming in, I knew I would have to close down the campaign. The Lord tested my faith in that area for sure.

At about 7:30 a.m. February 6, 1986, the finance committee (the new campaign manager, Tom, the treasurer, and I) met at an Embers restaurant in North St.Paul. Tom called the meeting to discuss a very important issue that we were facing.

The State Republican Convention was scheduled for the middle of June. We needed $10,000 by the close of that day if I was to stay in the race and we only had a couple of hundred bucks in the bank. On the other hand, we had so much going for us, and, at that point, it looked like we were winning.

We were seated off to the side of the restaurant, speaking in low voices to make sure no one heard what we were talking about. As we finished breakfast and our discussion, I saw a very tall man out of the corner of my eye approaching our table. Sure enough, he stopped at the table just long enough to look me squarely in the eye, quickly grabbed the bill off the table, and said five words. "It's going to be alright." We were all stunned. For some reason, I thought, there was something unusual about this man. We all felt it and just looked at each other. There was no way he could have heard our conversation because he came from a far corner of the restaurant. We were all a little stunned and saw him walk up to the register and pay our bill. None of us had ever seen him before.

Almost as quickly as he appeared, he seemed to disappear. Without hesitation, I jumped up, checked the bathroom, and ran outside. Surely he could not have reached his car in those few seconds. He was simply nowhere to be found.

I headed back into the restaurant. I met the manager and told him what had just happened, I said, "Fred, have you ever seen that man before?"

Fred said, "Nope, never saw him before, he paid cash."

I said to him "I tried to find him, I looked outside and it seemed as though he disappeared."

He said, "Mike, what are you talking about? He paid your tab maybe 30 or 45 minutes ago."

"No," I said. "That's impossible. He paid it no more than two minutes ago."

"Here, let me show you something," Fred said, shaking his head.

He explained that when customers paid their tabs he pushed the ticket on a nail-like spindle. He picked up the spindle and showed me that our receipt was about two-thirds of the way down and he pulled it out. Sure enough, our ticket was right there on the spindle.

"That proves it. That guy paid at least 45 minutes ago."

I thanked Fred, hoping he didn't think I was missing a cog in the wheels upstairs, and I went back to the table. The guys and I agreed it was unexplainable!

We had an election to win and the big question was would $10,000 come in the 11:00 a.m. morning mail? We were up against a deadline. We needed to pay our share of the convention hall where the convention would be held. We had to place an order for banners and other convention materials needed by the next day. The words of the strange, tall man kept ringing in my ear, "It's going to be alright."

I had several donor meetings that day and two other speaking engagements. I fully believed the money we needed would be in the mail that morning. I called the office a little before noon. I was clinging to the words of the tall man. I was beginning to wonder if he was an angel sent by God.

The campaign manager, Tom, answered the phone. I asked him what was in the mail. "Sorry, Mike, only a couple hundred in the mail."

I took a deep breath. "Let's believe the money comes today by some other means. The tall stranger said it was going to be alright, Tom, I believe what he said. There was just something special about the tall guy and the way he said it."

A peace began to settle over my mind. I felt deeply loved by God as if the tall stranger had showered some of God's love on me.

That was a promise from God; I'm sure of it, I kept thinking about that phrase as the day wore on. The passage from John 14:27 also kept ringing in my ears, "Peace I leave with you; my peace I give you. I do not give to you as the world gives. Do not let your hearts be troubled and do not be afraid." [NIV]

Late that afternoon I was sitting at my desk thinking about the campaign and my family. It was 5:00 p.m. when my campaign manager walked into my office with a peculiar look on his face. He laid a check for $10,000 on my desk, made out to the Menning for Governor Campaign. My belief in angels coming to minister to us has never wavered since that day!

The $10,000 given that day along with the couple of hundred that came in the mail that morning was enough to pay all the bills with a little money left over. If we are in God's will for our lives, it seems as though He is never early, and certainly is never late.

There was something special about the tall stranger that day. God cares for us and always will care for us. Yes, even in our darkest and most challenging times, we can count on the great and only God who loves us beyond measure and provides confirmations for us, sometimes in the most unusual ways.

Fundraising was an ever-present source of pressure in that statewide campaign. Campaigning for the endorsement of the party is far different than running in the general election. One of the big challenges in seeking the endorsement is maintaining a balance in reaching the potential delegates to the State Endorsing Convention and getting our supporters to run for and win those delegate positions. We also needed "earned media," or getting my name in the newspapers, on television, and radio so "our people" would hear about us. That would give them the confidence needed to continue supporting us. They needed to be able to hold their heads high in support of their candidate and believe things were moving in the right direction.

We had to get the message out to over 2,000 delegates about why I was running and where I stood on the issues. The delegates needed to be convinced that I was able to govern the state. Doing this in a large state like Minnesota was no small task. It meant careful planning to make the best use of my time and ensuring I would get to gatherings on time. We were very grateful to the people who flew me from city to city and town to town.

I knew it was important for the people of Minnesota to know our family outside of the political realm. One way that was accomplished was to get our book *Us Four: a Senator, His Family, Their Brain-Injured Child* into the hands of my supporters. One of our supporters purchased 1,000 copies and took it upon himself to mail the books to delegates throughout the state. This permitted them to meet our family, including Michael, without allowing him to become the focus of any negative press.

As the winter moved on it seemed as if I was working on the campaign day and night. I was counting the months, weeks, and days until the endorsing convention in June 1986.

I knew I needed to be careful in my choice of a running mate for the Lieutenant Governor position and needed to proceed with that soon. The decision was heavy on my mind. The person would have to be qualified to take over as governor should the need arise. The person also had to be someone who would be an asset to the ticket. I believed I knew just the guy for the job. He had served as the State Director of Development in the Governor Quie administration. I considered several others, but I had peace about this guy, and as a bonus, I considered him my brother in Christ.

I had five advisors that I considered my "Kitchen Cabinet." Four out of the five overwhelmingly agreed with my choice of Art Sidner to fill that position. One person on the committee was unable to attend the meeting when the final decision was made. Art was excited to join me as my running mate.

About a month before the convention, we decided to publicly announce the choice at a press conference. Some were astonished that I would choose a black man as my running mate. I think it was the first time an African American ran for a high office in Minnesota. I certainly didn't do it to gain the black vote because in those days there were not a lot of black people living in Minnesota.

On Saturday, I headed back home after the announcement. I arrived mid-evening after a very busy week. I was tired and looked forward to a good night of sleep. At about midnight the phone next to our bed rang and woke me from a deep sleep. I was startled, but I answered.

The voice on the other end of the line sounded agitated. He said who he was, but I didn't catch it. Then he repeated his name in a loud and angry voice, "This is Matt Casper!"

Matt was the one member of the Kitchen Cabinet who had missed the meeting a few days before.

"Yeah, Matt, what's going on? Why are you calling at this hour?"

He was very upset with my choice of Art Sidner as my running mate. "That n------- friend of yours will not be on the ballot."

My heart pounded as anger and shock flooded through my

body. "I am not going to continue this conversation. We will talk on Monday," and I hung up.

I seldom mixed campaign business with Sunday, my day of rest, worship, and family time, but that Sunday I called my campaign manager and told him about the midnight call. I asked him to set up a meeting with the Kitchen Cabinet.

It turned out that we couldn't get the group together until 10:30 on Monday night. I knew the meeting was going to be difficult. Matt Casper was seething with rage. He blurted out to everyone, "You can give your n— friend anything he wants after the election, but he will not be on the ticket."

I completely lost it. I pounded my fist on the flimsy portable table, pop cans went flying, and I lunged across the table at him. "You're off the committee," I yelled. "Get out of here, you are the worst racist I've ever met." It was unbelievable to me as he yelled more racist remarks on his way out of the room.

Casper's evil perspective was wrong, however, the way I responded was also wrong – losing control like that. He left the room that night white-hot with anger. He was determined to get back at me and destroy my political career. Within about a week, we began to see the results of the tongue-lashing I gave Matt Casper.

Soon, we were getting feedback from some of our delegates. All over the state, delegates were receiving calls from strange and unknown sources. These callers were dragging me through the mud, saying I was mentally unfit for public office, and lying about me. We knew it was an organized effort of Matt Casper, but I didn't understand how he had gathered so many people to make those hateful calls.

The Minnesota Republican Endorsing Convention was a few weeks away. We were getting slammed and couldn't imagine how the eleventh-hour smear campaign was organized. Our huge lead dwindled by the day.

It was mid-June and finally, the day of the convention arrived.

11

Our good friends, Pastor Dan DeGroot and his wife Mary flew with Michael to St. Paul in a private plane. Dawn and Mitchell came with relatives who attended.

By this time many of the delegates who supported me just six weeks earlier were confused and some began to believe the rumors started by the thousands of mysterious phone calls.

The convention started with much excitement, pomp, and circumstance. The campaigns of the three candidates left in the race for governor were in high gear. The speeches, demonstrations, and songs were over. The voting had begun. On the first ballot, each of the three candidates received approximately a third of the votes from the delegates.

The second and third ballots were taken and the Speaker of the House was picking up steam. I knew something had to be done to keep him from running off with the endorsement. I stood in the back, in a secluded area, and prayed. God was answering my prayer, but not the way I was expecting. I felt a peaceful message that it was time for me to pull out of the race. I knew I needed to ask my delegates to support my friend Cal Ludeman. *Lord,* I said, *I don't understand, but I know that you are in this. Please, Lord, help me to understand, is this really what I am to do?* I told Dawn, Mitch, my staff, and close friends around me that it was over. It was time to announce and ask my delegates to support Cal Ludeman.

There were 2,000 delegates present. Dawn, Mitch, and I started down the long convention hall aisle. Television cameras were ahead of us and behind us, all the way to the podium. As we went forward, many of our friends and delegates were crying.

I made the announcement, the next vote was taken, and Cal Ludeman won the endorsement to be the Republican candidate for governor. After a year and a half of hard work, speaking on what I believed, and organizing hundreds and even thousands of supporters around the state, within minutes my campaign for governor was over.

Sleep was hard to come by that night. I lay in the dark and it hit me. We had lived in a fishbowl for a year and a half. All that time it looked like I would have an opportunity to make huge changes in the state and now it was all over.

The next morning, I met with a few of our staff. Tom, the campaign manager, came into my office and dropped a bombshell.

"Mike, I need to tell you that I broke your rule of not spending more money than we had in the bank account. We spent more than we had. We knew you would understand once you got the endorsement."

"Tom, you didn't, how bad is it?"

"The campaign is $30,000 in debt."

With that, Tom left my office and packed up his belongings. I never heard or saw or heard from him again. I am sad to say, he disappeared from my life.

My secretary, Sally Quebodeaux, and a few others including my friend, Dave Racer, my first campaign manager, said they would close down the office and wrap up loose ends. They encouraged Dawn, the boys, and me to continue with our plans to go to a cabin we had reserved on a lake in northern Minnesota. The campaign debt was heavy on my mind.

Late that evening, we arrived at the cabin. Michael was with us. We got him in the cabin before we unloaded the car. The first thing he did was to go and turn on the TV. The news was on when I walked into the cabin. "Today, the State Senate Republican candidate running for Mike Menning's old senate seat has announced that he will withdraw from the race to allow Menning to get his old senate seat back." Wow, was I shocked!!

Within a few weeks, I was working to raise the $30,000 debt of the governor's race and announced that I would once again seek re-election for the State Senate. I raised $25,000 and added $5,000 from our meager savings account, and paid off the debt. However, I failed to win back my former seat in the Minnesota State Senate.

I believe it was God's will for me to be the candidate for governor. There was no doubt that God was in that race and if He wanted me to win I would have won. However, my thoughts were - *God doesn't always call us to be successful in the eyes of man. God does ask us to be faithful to His call. I believe I was faithful to His call.*

Over 20 years after the vicious telephone campaign against me, a friend sent me a newspaper clipping with a short article announcing that Matt Casper had died. There was his picture with fellow members of the Ku Klux Klan from the State of Alabama! We knew Matt was a racist but we never knew about this connection with the Klan until 20 years later. I firmly believe it was the Klan who had come into Minnesota to assist with the telephone campaign to destroy my campaign for governor, all because of their hatred for a good man who had black skin. To this day, I feel personally hurt when folks exhibit racism.

Cal Ludeman, the guy I supported at the convention, went on to run against incumbent Democrat, Rudy Perpich. When Rudy was lieutenant governor he and I had become good friends. Perpich won against Ludeman and was sworn in as governor the following January.

Three months after Perpich was sworn in, Dawn and I were sitting in the living room of our home with Mitch when the phone rang. Dawn called to me, "It's Rudy Perpich, he would like to talk to you."

I had sent him a note and apologized to him for some of the things I had said about him in the heat of the campaign. He said he had been carrying my letter in his lapel pocket for a couple of weeks and wanted to personally talk with me about that and a couple of other things. We had a good time talking, making up after our disagreements, and laughing like in old times.

Rudy shared with me that he was under incredible pressure from the press. My heart ached for the governor. I was honored that he knew he could trust me. I was willing to listen and encourage my friend, even though we were on opposite sides of the aisle politically.

When I hung up the phone and rejoined my family I will never forget what Mitch, an eighth-grader, said to me, "Dad, I sure am glad that you didn't win the governor's race."

"Why do you say that?"

"Because if you had won, I know you could be sitting in that office in the Governor's chair making those phone calls tonight and Mom and I would be at home without you."

That spoke volumes to me. Mitch knew what he was saying. He knew what the governor's office looked like because had been there with me as a child. I think it was God who kept me from becoming Minnesota Governor. God put me to the test to trust Him and only Him and to be faithful to His call.

***

During my governor's race, one of the staff people we hired was a guy named Tony. He was a young attorney in his late twenties. He was a bright guy and an asset to the campaign. He traveled with me and often attended fundraisers and other events in the Twin Cities area. I got to know Tony quite well and soon became aware that even though he told a good story about being a believer, it was quite obvious he had not given his life to Jesus.

On several occasions, I shared with Tony what it was to be serious about making a solid commitment to Jesus. I told him about the need for repentance of sins, to confess to God that he believed that Jesus was the Son of God. He needed to accept Jesus as his personal Savior and to fully live for the Master.

Tony just didn't seem to fully understand what I shared with him. Or was he too stubborn? After I lost the endorsement, Tony and I lost contact.

A few years passed. On a very cold Sunday night in January at about midnight, I was awakened when the bedroom phone interrupted our sleep. I thought, *did someone die?*

"Hello?"

"Mike, this is Tony." I knew right away the Tony I was talking to, despite his voice sounding ragged.

"Tony, what's going on?"

He explained that his life was in shambles. He said that morning he had been invited by his brother-in-law to attend a church service. "That preacher was preaching right to me, no one else in the church, directly to me. I'm not kidding."

The preacher's message was that when a person loses everything of importance to him and reaches the bottom, the only way out is to give his life to Jesus and watch Jesus help him put things back together again. Tony was angry and decided not to listen to that preacher anymore. He tried to stand up and leave the service, but it was like he was paralyzed. "Mike, I couldn't move," he said between sobs and sniffles. "I had to just sit there and listen."

I pulled on a pair of jeans, turned up the thermostat, and went to the dining room of our home as I didn't want to keep Dawn awake. Tony poured out his guts to me and I finally got him settled down. "Mike, a few years ago you told me how to accept Jesus. I need to do that," he blurted. "Can you read those verses from the Bible that you read to me before, you know, during the campaign?"

"Yeah, sure Tony, but I need to get my Bible. It's in the car and my car is outside beside the house. We are in the middle of a snowstorm here. Hold on, Tony. Give me a couple of minutes and I'll be right back."

We lived in the country on top of a hill. The wind was howling and blowing, I'm guessing at about 40 mph with a wind chill of maybe -50F. In the blowing snow, I headed out of the house to get my favorite marked-up Bible. I could barely see my hand in front of my face. I figured if this guy called me in the middle of the night to ask me how to accept Jesus, this snowstorm wouldn't stop me.

I got back in the house and was thinking of that scripture about being ready to share the gospel at all times, now, let's see, where is that found again? 2 Timothy 2:4, "Preach the word; be prepared in season and out of season; correct, rebuke and encourage—with great patience and careful instruction." [NIV] I shared the promises of the Scripture with Tony, including Romans 10:9, "If you declare with your mouth, 'Jesus is Lord,' and believe in your heart that God raised him from the dead, you will be saved." [NIV] That night, Tony prayed to receive Jesus as his personal Savior. An hour and a half later, I got back into bed.

Dawn awoke and looked at the clock. "Have you been talking to Tony all this time?"

"Yep."

"What did he want that was so urgent?"

"Oh, he wanted to know how to give his life to Jesus."

"At this hour?"

"Yep. I'll tell you more in the morning," I smiled.

The next morning, we had an enjoyable breakfast conversation! I also told Dawn that I would be calling my friend Randy Kroll who lived north of the Twin Cities, and ask him to start mentoring my old friend Tony, who was now a brother in Jesus.

I got to thinking, I lost the campaign for governor, but it was through the campaign that I got to know Tony. And now, I had the privilege of leading him to Christ. It was all worth it.

An ambassador of Jesus always has time, even in the middle of the night in a Minnesota blizzard, to share as the old song goes, "I love to tell the story, the old, old story of Jesus and His glory, of Jesus and His love."

Two

Challenges and Fifteen Wonderful Years

For we are his workmanship, created in Christ Jesus
for good works, which God prepared
beforehand, that we should walk in them.
Ephesians 2:10 [ESV]

The seven-month period from mid-June 1986 until the middle of January 1987 was a very difficult time for me. In June of '86, I lost my bid for the Republican nomination for governor. In November of the same year, I lost the bid trying to win back my old senate seat. Dawn worked tirelessly on that senate race and was deeply hurt by the loss. Life for us was challenging. Once again, God was testing us.

Kent George, my opponent in the race for the senate seat, was a proud and difficult man. Often the two people running for the same political office get to know the real heart and character of each other.

One day while campaigning, I was knocking on doors in his hometown. A lady opened the door. She and her daughter invited me in. I knew there was something special about these people; I guess it was the way they listened when I spoke. They seemed to be calm, gentle people, and I could feel the presence of the Lord in that apartment. Then she told me that she was my opponent's first wife and that she and her daughters were now Christians.

She told me that after the divorce she and Kent remarried. A couple of years after they were remarried, she met Jesus and accepted Him as her personal Savior. At that point, her husband divorced her a second time. He was avidly anti-Christian.

A couple of months before the election my opponent made wild promises to farmers in our district, although he knew he could not carry out the commitments. He and a few of his radical farmer friends, one from my church, pushed a misleading issue across the Senate District. It was hard times for many in the mid-80s, but my opponent saw a real opportunity to take advantage of the situation.

I lost the election. The newly elected senator never looked back at the promises he made but carried on as though nothing happened. While serving in public office, as in many other areas, life often proves to be difficult. I learned that it is so much better to forgive, love the person who wronged me, and move on.

***

Within a day or two after losing the senate race, I was contacted by a regional non-profit organization asking if I would be interested in applying for the job of director. I had given part of my life to this organization, and it was close to my heart. I figured it could be a perfect fit for me.

I had several meetings with the board and the founders. They hired me under the condition that I would raise the funds for my salary. God miraculously provided 25% of the total needed for my annual salary through one donor, and I got started in my new role. Dawn was invited to work as a volunteer with me. I soon found that it was very difficult working under the founder who said she would be backing out. Quite the opposite was true. She wanted to micromanage and run my schedule.

Within a few weeks, I found that major changes would have

19

to be made, especially in the handling of the finances. The money management was questionable, both ethically and legally. I gathered the information for the board explaining that I needed the authority to make 13 major changes or I would have to terminate my relationship with the organization.

At the January board meeting, I presented my findings to the Board of Trustees. Wow, did that ever backfire on me! The chairman of the board was the husband of the founder, and told me that I couldn't quit because I was fired. With that, I packed up my things and left. This was good news for the founder because she refused to return the money I had raised for my salary and expenses.

Once again, I needed to forgive and move on. We don't always get justice in this life, however, if we ask God, he can and does turn those bad times into something good. "We know that for those who love God, all things work together for good, for those who are called according to his purpose." Romans 8:28 [ESV]

There I was, unemployed. In the seven months prior, I lost two elections and was fired from a job for the first time in my life. Even when I was knocked down, through the power of the Holy Spirit, I found I could get up, dust myself off, go forward, and trust God all the way. I received strength from the Holy Spirit to move on.

I went home and spent time with the Lord. For the first time in my life, I needed to put together a resume. Times had changed and I found my new way of life hard to deal with. Dawn was a great help and I appreciated it. Also, for the first time in my life, I spent time on a job search and quickly got the message that companies were not willing to touch me, a former and somewhat well-known political figure. The rejections piled up, weighing heavily on my bruised spirit.

Those were hard times for us, especially for Dawn. She had worked so hard in the last senate race and now it seemed as though the Lord had abandoned us. Our Pastor Dan De Groot came over and listened to our inmost thoughts and feelings. He gave us good advice and reassured us that our Lord had not left us and that God had plans for us.

Dan asked how we were doing financially. We had been very careful about our spending and had a savings account that could carry us for several months. We were also almost four years ahead on payments for our small farm. He suggested that I not aggressively look for a job. Instead, he recommended that I should take some time off and spend much time in prayer, every day, and trust the Lord. Great advice. We took it to heart.

Dawn went back to the job for $4.50 an hour at New Life Treatment Center, a Christian alcohol and drug treatment center. She served as an assistant to the director, Wes Van Essen, a good friend of ours. She loved the mission of the Center and enjoyed the work environment.

God was working on my heart asking me to trust Him fully. Every morning for two months, shortly after Dawn left for work, I got on my knees in front of the couch in the living room and spent time in prayer. Those times were precious and I have cherished them for the rest of my life.

To this day, I take time every day to be with the Lord. God pressed on my heart that I needed to wait on Him and He would give me work that He prepared in advance for me to do. "For we are his workmanship, created in Christ Jesus for good works, which God prepared beforehand, that we should walk in them." Ephesians 2:10 [ESV]

Waiting on the Lord during this season challenged me to my core. I was always busy with what I was supposed to be doing. As Henry T. Blackaby taught, God is not as concerned about what we do, but more about our heart as we do it. We should wait on God so He can show us His heart. I was learning not to just get on with **doing.**

***

21

In March of 1987, two months later, some would say *out of nowhere*, the much-anticipated call came. "Hello," the voice on the other end of the line said, "Is this Mike Menning?"

"Yes, it is."

"This is Andy Ryskamp from the Christian Reformed World Relief Committee (CRWRC). I am sure you know Pete Boer of Edgerton, one of our board members."

"Yes, I do."

"He recommended I call you and talk to you about a ministry position we have open. We would prefer to hire someone from the Midwest." He went on to explain that the person's job description would be to head up a ministry as a denominational employee for the Christian Reformed Church. "Mike, can I take a few minutes of your time to talk about this?"

"Sure, good to talk with you, Andy."

I tried not to let on, but my heart was pounding. *Wow, God, this could be the call!*

Andy went on to say that the person in this position would be working with deacons in four classes. (A classis is a geographic area with eight to twelve Christian Reformed Churches.) He went on to say that Edgerton was very centrally located. I thought, *wow, can you believe it?*

Several years before I prayed the Biblical account of the Prayer of Jabez, as found in 1 Chronicles 4:9-10. There was no doubt God heard that prayer, and my territory was already greatly expanded. I believed God had this offer in mind all along. God often keeps us in the waiting room for a longer time than we anticipate. He tests us to see if we trust Him.

I was very interested and filled out the application. The interview process was a long one. The last step was that Dawn and I needed to fly to Grand Rapids, Michigan to meet with Andy at the Christian

Reformed Church (CRC) Denominational Headquarters.

Both of us were required to take a psychological exam. I was interviewed in his office and could tell, without a doubt, that the distinguished Doctor of Psychiatry didn't like me – it was apparent that he had little time for those who had served in public office. He even made a few nasty comments about the legislative process. It felt like he was attacking me. The entire process took four hours and I was exhausted when it was over.

Dawn was waiting for me after the interview. "Let's go back to the hotel, pack up and head for home. That was the worst interview I have ever experienced," I said.

She replied, "No, we are staying to wrap up our noon appointment tomorrow with Andy." She was right, as usual.

When Andy came to meet with us, he had a nervous chuckle and a curious look in his eyes that I grew to know well in the coming years. The psychiatrist was not recommending me, so I was correct in my assessment of this guy from my interview. Later, Andy told me what he had said about me, "I wouldn't touch this guy with a ten-foot pole."

Andy wanted to hire me, but the Executive Director John DeHaan said the only way he could agree was if I would go through a second psychological assessment with a different psychiatrist. He suggested that I be examined by the psychologist they used for hiring foreign field staff. I would need to go through the process for another four hours that same afternoon. I did and it went very well. I emerged from the lengthy interview and gave Dawn a thumbs up.

I could immediately see that Andy's countenance had changed as he entered the room. He told us that the second psychologist had given him the opposite report and highly recommended me for the position. "So, Mike, you have the job if you want it." Wow! I was excited and so was Dawn!

I had a job in full-time ministry and I was pumped. Dawn knew me well and knew it would be a good fit. Andy said I would have to promise to give CRWRC a minimum of three years. I said I would be honored to take the job. The direction of my life changed.

One of my favorite Scripture passages, Psalm 139:16 says, "Your eyes saw my unformed body; all the days ordained for me were written in your book before one of them came to be." [NIV] God had a plan for my life and I was walking through the doors He opened for me.

It turned out that working for CRWRC for fifteen years was one of the greatest experiences of my life. God used this wonderful opportunity in ways for which I cannot give Him enough thanks and praise. He used me to help develop many others in ministry as well. Andy Ryskamp was the greatest boss anyone could ever hope to have. He taught me much about leadership development and led me from some of my narrow thinking.

During this time, I was also able to complete my Master's Degree from Azusa Pacific University.

For the first ten years with CRWRC, I mentored and taught deacons from many churches, mostly in Minnesota, Iowa, and South Dakota, and a few in Wisconsin, Arizona, Kansas, and Texas. In some churches, deacons had become the bookkeepers and finance directors of the church, and that's all. I helped and encouraged them to move back into the practice of carrying out the Biblical mandate of the office of deacon, to care for the poor, both monetarily and spiritually, in their churches and their communities. I worked with many wonderful teams of people both in the US and Canada.

I loved my work more than anything I had ever done and felt fulfilled in my calling to serve the Lord. There was never a dull day. I felt peace in my heart and my whole being as I was in this full-time ministry and was maturing as an ambassador of Jesus. My official title was "Process Consultant." During the last five years with CRWRC, I served as Team Leader for their ministry in Eastern Europe.

Three

60 Miles to the South

And he (God) determined the times set for them
and the exact places they should live.
Acts 17:26b [NIV 1984]

Michael was twenty years old and had been living in a Hope Haven group home in Rock Valley, Iowa for a few years. It was his home, except on weekends when he joined us in Edgerton. But we were becoming concerned about his future.

Under Minnesota law, the school district was responsible for the cost of Michael's education. However, when he turned 21, Minnesota law required that he return to Minnesota and he would need to receive services in a Minnesota care facility. We looked at a few of the Minnesota facilities. At the time it seemed the best options in Minnesota were in either Worthington, 45 minutes away, or Mankato, 110 miles away.

Not only did Hope Haven provide the best of services, but it was a Christ-centered organization, providing Christ-like love and care for Michael. We knew beyond a shadow of a doubt the best option for Michael's future was for us to move to his new hometown and establish Iowa residency in Rock Valley. Moving was a big deal for us even though we already knew many fine people there. We had a difficult time making the decision. One of the biggest concerns was Dawn's mom, Gram Den Ouden who was such an integral part of our family. We saw her every day, and she walked life with us. We knew that if it was better for Michael, she would support our decision, and that is precisely what she did.

In the winter of 1993, Dawn was on an annual ministry trip to Voice of Calvary Ministries in Jackson, Mississippi. Justice For All is a ministry that had been founded years before by folks from Rock Valley. The group she was with were friends of ours. I was home in Edgerton with Michael for the weekend. The plan was for me to take him back to Rock Valley for Sunday morning worship. He and I attended the Trinity Christian Reformed Church in Rock Valley. It was about halfway through that service that the Lord made it clear in my mind; we needed to move to Rock Valley.

The service was over and I talked with some people in the congregation. I was surprised by how many people I knew. I was feeling warmth and peace about the church and the possibility of making Rock Valley our home. When I brought Michael back to his home I asked him a question before I left. "Well Michael, do you think Mom and Dad should move to Rock Valley and live in your town?" He seemed to understand, nodded, and gave me a big smile. As I was leaving the group home and walking down the sidewalk returning to my car, something was different, really different. I had peace about moving to Rock Valley. I was reminded of Acts 17:26b, the apostle Paul wrote, "And he (God) determined the times set for them (we) and the exact places they should live." [NIV 1984]

How would Dawn react? I decided to call her. Much to my surprise, and perhaps hers, she was favorable to the idea that it was a very real possibility for our family and could be a good thing for all of us. She had peace in her mind about the possibility of moving. It meant we would move from our home community and state, the place where we were born, raised, and loved. Rock Valley, Iowa, would become our new hometown. We felt it was the best for Michael and we liked the idea. Rock Valley was a healthy community with a population of a bit less than 3,000.

Within a week, we started making plans including visiting with a realtor from Rock Valley. At that time there were only two houses for sale in the entire town. God continued to lead us. There was an empty lot on the first fairway of the golf course, so we could build a new house. The realtor talked to the owner, and he gave us a price that we thought was reasonable. We decided to purchase the lot and build a new house.

We chose the son-in-law of our good friends, Wes and Jean Van Essen, to design the house and draw up the architectural plans. We liked other houses he had designed. The process took longer than anticipated, but in the end, we were very happy with the plans and the design.

The next step in this process was to find a contractor from Rock Valley to build the house. We found that all the contractors were booked out for the next six to eight months. I also talked with contractors from nearby Sioux Center, Iowa, all to no avail. I decided to be the general contractor for the project which meant I would hire subcontractors to do the various pieces involved in the building of the house. For the most part, that worked very well.

There is an old saying, "If your marriage can survive the building of a home, it can handle anything." Our marriage survived. Our house was framed by the men who usually framed for that architect we used. We hired our good friends Stan DeWeerd and Mike Harmsen to wire and plumb the house in the evenings and on Saturdays. Mitch, his buddy Kirk, and I did much of the sheetrock during the Dordt College Christmas break. I was able to find a person to do the mudding and texturing of the sheetrock. I rented a sprayer and painted the entire house myself. Dawn painted some of the accent walls. A local contractor, Floyd Davelaar, built all the solid oak cabinets and did an exquisite job.

Our move in December 1993 from Edgerton was treacherous, including nearly slipping into the ditch on solid black-ice roads. We got moved into a rental house a few days before Christmas. It allowed us to be close and available to assist in whatever way we could to get the new house finished.

By the end of March 1994, we moved into our new home and loved it.

Michael lived just across town, about a mile and a half from our home. The trips getting Michael home for the weekends now took only a few minutes. We loved our new church home and the culture of the community. I thought we could slip into the new community and new state without much fanfare, but we were in for a surprise. A couple of weeks after we moved, the local newspaper had a front-page story with the headline something like "Former Minnesota Senator Menning Moves to Rock Valley."

One of the unique things about this little Dutch community was the fact that there were few social cliques. The bankers, truck drivers, medical community, factory workers, teachers, business people, farmers, and many more all mixed and mingled with each other. There were exceptions of course, but, for the most part, one group of people didn't think more highly of themselves than another.

Our time in Rock Valley proved to be very special in our lives, and was undoubtedly all a part of God's plan for our lives. The friendships developed in that great little community were many; they were sincere and grew deep. Little did we know at the time that many of these friendships would last for the rest of our lives. One of the most unique cultural attributes of the community was their incredible care and love for people with disabilities.

***

One of our memorable experiences while living in Rock Valley was when United States Presidential Candidate Lamar Alexander and his wife, Honey, stayed in our home overnight. Lamar and I had something special in common since we both had run for governor, me in Minnesota and he in Tennessee. However, we differed in one major area - he won the governor's race in Tennessee and I lost my governor's race in Minnesota. Governor Alexander went on to serve honorably for two terms. He then went on to serve as President Ronald Reagan's Secretary of Education. In 1996 he ran for the Republican nomination for President of the United States. That's when we reconnected in Iowa.

During an early visit, I drove him from town to town for a couple of days. I felt good about serving on his campaign and we had many great talks in the car traveling from event to event. Iowa was always a very important state for any Republican presidential candidate, as it was the first state in the Union to hold political caucuses. Rock Valley is located in Sioux County and I am told that it is perhaps the strongest Republican county in the nation.

On another of his visits to Northwest Iowa, we decided to sponsor an open house in our home for *Alexander for President* on a Sunday evening after our worship service. The turnout was greater than anticipated. There was standing room only in our home. People were standing outside on our driveway sidewalk and front lawn waiting to meet him and hear what he had to say. I remember he stood on a chair in our living room to give his speech. Then he went outside, stood on the front porch, and spoke to those gathered outside. After the crowds left we had a relaxing time sipping decaf coffee and munching a few snacks. Looking back, it was hard to believe that possibly the next President of the United States and his bride, the First Lady, were guests in our home. When I prayed the prayer of Jabez, many years earlier, I asked God to expand my territory and God was surely faithful to my prayer.

About a month earlier George W. Bush had jumped into the race. The Bush machine was hard to compete with and was coming on strong. That evening Lamar shared with us that the Bush Campaign was drying up his prospective funds. After we retired for the night, Dawn said, "Did you notice Honey? Did you listen to her? I think this race is about over."

Dawn read Honey correctly. About a week later, I was invited to join a conference call with some of the campaign volunteers and staff. Lamar announced that he was dropping out of the race. I was sad, but like my governor's race, God had other plans.

***

So, I have asked, why the Rock Valley experience? Here are just a few ways God worked in our lives. For one thing, Michael was able to continue his wonderful life at Hope Haven while we lived in Iowa. We got to know leaders from Hope Haven with whom we later traveled to Romania to introduce them to people in the Eastern Bloc after Communism. Hope Haven went on to establish Christ-centered programs, not only in Romania, but in many other countries as well. Dawn served as a consultant with Hope Haven Romania for several years.

Years later, friends we made in Rock Valley and a few churches from that area became some of the greatest prayer and financial supporters for the Great Commission Utah ministry. This was without a doubt all in God's plan.

I am a country boy at heart. God moved us from Edgerton to Rock Valley, a community three times larger than Edgerton. Rock Valley had one stoplight and I didn't particularly appreciate it. Strange and maybe a bit off the wall as it may seem, the wonderful Rock Valley experience prepared our family in many ways for another move God had in store for us; a move to Salt Lake City, Utah.

Now, do you see how God sometimes works; even in the small things of life?

Reflections & Pondering

So we are Christ's ambassadors; God is making his appeal through
us. We speak for Christ when we plead,
"Come back to God."
2 Corinthians 5:20 [NLT]

Reflections on <u>Your</u> Life

Many Biblical characters experienced what is called the death of a vision, for example, Abraham and Sarah struggled to think that their hope of having a baby was over. Consider Jacob, he looked forward to a great life ahead but he had many, many challenges. As a teenager, Jacob's favorite son, Joseph, looked ahead, shared his dreams that almost cost him his life, and was sold into slavery in Egypt. Moses anticipated entering the promised land but was not allowed to enter, because of the sin he committed in not speaking to the rock, he struck the rock.

Mike later said that doing God's will doesn't necessarily mean becoming successful in the eyes of man, but to follow God's will for your life. Why do think God took Mike that far and then allowed him to lose the endorsement race in the Governor's campaign? Can you think of any good that came out of the loss of that election?

The Mennings experienced the death of the vision of two healthy children, Mike lost the governor's race, he lost the election of getting back his old senate seat, and he was unjustly fired as director of a non-profit ministry. Another death of a vision was experienced by the

Alexanders. Can you think of examples in your life when God closed a window but He opened a door? What "death of a vision" have you experienced and what doors did God open?

"And he (God) determined the times set for them (us) and the exact places they should live." Acts 17:26b [NIV 1984 translation] Do you think you are living where God wants you to live and are you doing what God wants you to do?

Check out Jeremiah 29:11 and Psalm 139:16. Mike went through hard times seeking God's will for his life. God has plans for His people. Are you doing what you think God has chosen for you?

What are ways of finding out what God has planned for you and your family?

Do you have other questions or comments about the stories in Chapters 1, 2, or 3?

Pondering <u>Your</u> Life's Direction

Did anything in chapters 1, 2, and 3 cause you to consider making a **change in your heart**?

Are there **Life Changes** you need to make to mature as an *ambassador of Jesus*?

Section Two

Incredible Joy and the Big Move

Four

Eastern Europe and the Joy of Evangelism

We are therefore Christ's ambassadors, as though God were making
his appeal through us. We implore you on Christ's behalf:
Be reconciled to God.
John 14:27 [NIV]

Don't forget these small beginnings, for the Lord rejoices
to see the work begin...
Zechariah 4:10 [NLT]

In the early 1990s, while serving as chair of Joni and Friends (JAF), I went to Eastern Europe with their international ministry.

At age sixteen Joni Eareckson Tada was injured in a diving accident that left her with quadriplegia, paralysis of all four limbs. Her books ministered to Dawn and me in amazing ways on our journey with Michael. I had an opportunity to meet her when I was in the Senate. I was later invited to serve on the board of JAF which ministered to and served people with disabilities all over the world. On my first trip to Romania, we taught leaders of Christian churches about their Biblical responsibility to care for people with disabilities. I was very touched when I saw the great needs of people with disabilities in Eastern Europe, especially in Romania.

When Dawn and I went to distribute wheelchairs in 1995, we

discovered that Romania had the highest abortion rate in the world. I knew something had to be done. After the overthrow of communism, women were told that they had the right over their bodies, including the future of their pregnancy and their unborn babies. For many the lack of education multiplied their problems.

God has often spoken to me while I have been on a trip. This is what I call "trip theology." This concept is very Biblical. Think about the trips of Abraham, Jacob, Joseph, Moses – and Jonah. Consider when God spoke to David when he was away from home on a trip to visit his brothers — he took out the giant Goliath! Many times Jesus took his disciples "away" from their homes and regular work, and then He taught them.

***

PEOPLE FROM SMALL PLACES – God often uses people from small places. Do you remember in the previous chapter that I told about how Pete Boer had recommended me for the new ministry position that was open in Christian Reformed World Relief? God used Pete Boer, a farmer and truck driver from the small community of Edgerton, Minnesota, to help bring about a small part of the ushering in of His Kingdom in various parts of the world. God spoke to Pete Boer while attending a CRWRC board meeting in Grand Rapids, Michigan – "trip theology" in action. I believe God nudged Pete Boer to recommend my name. Pete responded to the nudge and talked to Andy Rykamp recommending that he contact me regarding the full-time ministry position.

The Apostle Paul said in I Corinthians 3:6, "I planted, Apollos watered, but God gave growth." [ESV] Pete planted the seed, Andy watered, and God made the seed, (me) grow as a sapling, the sapling grew into a tree and the tree produced fruit; the fruit produced more seeds, and perhaps more seeds around the world took root, and started all over again – all orchestrated by the mighty hand of God.

Did Pete have any idea at that time how many people around the world would eventually come to the Lord through his faithfulness as an ambassador of Jesus? Of course, he didn't know. He was being faithful to the voice of the Shepherd. When I was hired I was serving as an ambassador of Jesus.

Later I will tell stories of how God used me as a tool in His hands to teach deacons how to become ambassadors of Him. God allowed me to be used in other countries, Romania, Somalia, and even in the amazing miracle of the release of the Gjakova, Kosovo 81 prisoners of war. I was used as a tool in the hand of God working with many church planters in Utah, and later establishing ministries to help people in the polygamist culture of Utah.

Where did this all start? It started with God working in the heart of a farmer from this small community – Pete Boer was an ambassador of Jesus! Another man of the soil was the author of one of the twelve minor prophet books of the Bible, his name was Amos. Pete and Amos were humble men of God, both followed the will of God in their lives and both were farmers. Let us not forget the words of Zechariah, as recorded in the 4th chapter, verse 10, "Don't forget these small beginnings, for the Lord rejoices to see the work begin,.." [NLT]

*** *

I made a proposal to the International Board of CRWRC asking for approval to open a new diaconal ministry in Romania. My vision was to establish a diaconal ministry in Eastern Europe. There would be three parts to the proposed mission of this new ministry.

First, we needed to establish effective pregnancy resource centers. Second, we needed to establish additional ministries for those people in the region who had disabilities. Finally, we needed to assist in teaching church leaders how to care for the poor in and around their communities.

After about a year, I was permitted to start the ministry under specific conditions. I had to raise funds for the Eastern Europe Ministry and carry on my regular work with deacons in the United States. I accepted the challenge and although it wasn't easy, the first year went well.

In 1996 I made my first trip to Romania with CRWRC to begin building the framework for a new ministry in that country. I hired the first staff person, someone I had known for a couple of years, Gabi Achim. He was a bright and godly young man. Gabi was a leader and became our "boots-on-the-ground" person. Gabi and I added qualified Christians as additional staff members. The wheels began turning and the Romanian ministry was born.

The plan was that I would continue to live in the U.S., however I was to commute to and from Eastern Europe four times a year. I stayed for two and sometimes three weeks at a time. Our goal was to have this ministry led by nationals. We believed the ministry leaders would develop more quickly by not having a North American leader present all the time. CRWRC granted me five years to fully develop the ministry to a point when the national staff could take over.

***

A highlight of my time in Eastern Europe was when God used me to negotiate the release of the 81 prisoners of war from Gjakova, Kosovo held in Serbia.

In 1999, the Kosovo War finally came to an end. This war had ground on for years until the U.S. military came to the aid of the Albanians living in Kosovo. The Serbs claimed to be Christian, but their actions were far from Christ-like. It was a brutal war. The U.S. military almost wiped out the Serb influence in the area and also destroyed much of Serbia's infrastructure. The U.S. and the United

Nations demanded that the Serbian Dictator Milosevic be brought to The Hague to stand trial in the International Court. In the meantime, Serbia released all Kosovo prisoners of war, except 81 of them from the small city of Gjakova. The Serbs hated the people of Gjakova because they were fierce fighters.

An agreement with the United Nations allowed CRWRC to work in Gjakova at the time. When I came to review the work of our CRWRC staff there, they were very excited to show me a new program they had established. The team was helping the Gjakova families of the prisoners of war being held in Serbian prison camps. The goal was to establish small businesses, so those families could make enough money to pay for the care of their family members held in the prison camps in Serbia.

Our staff was somewhat surprised when they saw that I was not so impressed with their program. "We need to get these guys out of prison and back to their families," I said.

"Oh sure, Mike, right, that would take an act of Congress," was their response.

"That's right," I responded, "and with the help of God, it can be done." I explained that the foreign aid package was at that very time being debated in the U.S. Congress. The bill contained a provision that said **NO** aid from the United States could go to Serbia. No aid would be released until the brutal dictator Milosevic was behind bars in The Hague. He then would be tried in the World Court for the atrocities he had committed against the Albanians living in Kosovo. I explained there needed to be an amendment to the foreign aid package saying that the "Gjakova 81," as they were called, must be released as a pre-condition for U.S. aid to be released to Serbia.

When I returned to the States I called my supervisor, Andy Ryskamp, and explained the situation to him. I asked if I could take time to prepare my case for key members of Congress and go to Washington D.C. to lead the way for an amendment to be placed on the foreign aid bill. Andy permitted me to go forward with this pursuit. It took a week to prepare the material. Dawn prepared the materials to tell the story in a simple, straightforward way so members of Congress could understand this complicated situation and hopefully find a solution to the problem. That week I also worked to get appointments set up with congressmen and/or their chiefs of staff. Congressman Ehlers from Grand Rapids, Michigan was of great help. I know that God sent the Holy Spirit ahead to prepare my way.

I flew to Washington D.C. and had breakfast in the House dining room with key members of Congress including members of the Albanian Caucus and the Foreign Relations Committee. This meeting was arranged by a congressman from Minnesota with whom I had previously served while in the State Senate. They told me that I needed a "buy-in" from the Kosovo Desk and the Serbia Desk at the State Department.

Until that week in Washington D.C., I knew very little about the inside workings of the U.S. State Department. I quickly discovered the meaning of "Kosovo Desk" and "Serbia Desk." Inside the massive U.S. State Department Building, there are offices for every country in the world. Each country of the world is represented by a U.S. Chief who is an expert on all that is happening in that particular country. My job was to speak with the chiefs of the Kosovo Desk, the Serbian Desk, and the Albanian Desk to get all three to agree to the proposed amendment to the Foreign Aid Bill. The bill was being debated in various congressional committees that exact week. I soon learned that timing was everything!

For four days I shuttled back and forth between the congressional offices and the State Department. I finally got the right people from Congress and the State Department to sign off on the agreed-on language. The amendment was placed in the bill and by Friday afternoon, the amended Foreign Aid Bill passed as amended by the House and moved on to the Senate.

God used my acquaintance with U.S. Senator Lamar Alexander to carry out His plan for the release of the Gjakova 81. The former governor of Tennessee, presidential candidate, who was then a U.S. Senator, led the charge in the Senate. The Senate agreed to the amendments and the next week President George W. Bush signed the Foreign Aid Bill into law. The language of the bill specifically stated that Serbia would get no foreign aid from the United States until the Gjakova 81 were released from prison and returned to their hometown of Gjakova, Kosovo. The next day the Gjakova 81 were on buses, headed for their homes in Kosovo!

I was simply a tool in the hands of God in getting those prisoners of war released and sent home. The families no longer had to pay the Serbian government to give their loved ones food in the Serbian prison.

A month later on my return trip to Kosovo, I knew our staff was very excited about a surprise they had planned for me. Unknown to me, the 81 prisoners of war were notified that I was returning to Gjakova. The staff planned a reception to honor me for the work I did to gain their release and provide an opportunity for me to meet some of the former prisoners of war.

Dawn came with me on that trip and we went to the gathering place only to find out that only one of the Gjakova 81 returned to thank me. The staff was very discouraged and apologized over and over. "How can it be that only one out of the 81 showed up?"

I reminded them of the story when Christ healed the ten lepers. "Now on his way to Jerusalem, Jesus traveled along the border between Samaria and Galilee. As he was going into a village, ten men who had leprosy met him. They stood at a distance and called out in a loud voice, 'Jesus, Master, have pity on us?' When he saw them, he said, 'Go, show yourselves to the priests.' And as they went, they were cleansed. One of them, when he saw he was healed, came back, praising God in a loud voice. He threw himself at Jesus' feet and thanked him – and he was a Samaritan." Luke 17:11-17 [NIV]

I said, "Don't forget it's God who wants to use us as tools in his hand to bring about His plans. Jesus got thanks from one out of ten, and I got one out of 81. I praised God for the one."

***

I began having severe health problems a couple of years later and was diagnosed with stress-onset diabetes. I believe the diagnosis could have resulted from the fact that I was often working 60 to 70 hours a week. My pancreas simply gave out. I was placed on medication and several years later needed to move to insulin.

In 2000 my health was again declining and I became extremely weak. After meeting with several doctors, it was suggested that I go to the Mayo Clinic in Rochester, Minnesota. After many examinations, I was diagnosed with Chronic Fatigue Syndrome. I was informed that only a very small percentage of patients ever fully recover. At one point I was so weak I had difficulty walking from the bedroom to the dining room to eat.

Slowly God began to grant healing to me. Many people, those who knew me and especially Christians in Romania, joined in fervent prayer for my healing and recovery. I needed to go for another consultation with my medical team at Mayo. My doctor had earlier mentioned staying away from anything in my food or drink that contained aspartame, I did so. She also recommended, "When you hit the glass ceiling, push yourself just a little further." At that visit she gave me the go-ahead to return to my work in Eastern Europe for two weeks. In the coming months, I began regaining strength, and I felt that if at all possible I needed to return to check on the work in Romania and Eastern Europe.

It had been nearly six months since I had been in my office in Bucharest. I wanted to return to Gabi, Glennis, Noemi, Doci, and other staff in Bucharest and Cluj/Napoca. (Mind you, Noemi later married our best friend's son, Scott, and became like a daughter to me.) Of course, I also missed seeing other ministry leaders, pastors, and a few members of Parliament.

I was slowly gaining strength and arrangements were made for my trip. Airline tickets were ordered, and I began gathering materials and clothing needed for the trip, the same flight I had taken many times. My bags were packed the day before departure. I had to be up by 4:00 the next morning. Dawn planned to take me to the regional airport in Sioux Falls, South Dakota to catch a 7:00 a.m. flight to Minneapolis, with continued travel to Amsterdam, and then on to Bucharest, Romania.

The afternoon before I left, I became extremely fatigued again. I didn't want to believe it, but, by four o'clock, I was exhausted. I figured it was just the excitement and anticipation of returning to Romania. I took a nap, got up, and didn't feel rested – my worst fears were becoming a reality. The sharp ringing in my ears had returned and my limbs were feeling very weak. Had the Chronic Fatigue come back with a vengeance? I hardly dared to voice the question. This whole trip had been covered in prayer, it simply couldn't be true. The doctor had given me the nod of approval and I was ready to go. But more than that, God had given me peace and seemed to tell us that I could return to the work I loved.

Dawn and I talked that evening and we decided that I would not cancel the trip. I went to bed and the next morning I was up early. By the time I got in the car, I was feeling very weak – my arms and legs felt weak and floppy and seemed like they weighed twenty pounds each. I trusted the Lord and decided to go ahead as planned. When we arrived at the airport we prayed in the car, and I kissed Dawn goodbye. She helped me get my bags out of the trunk, and I was able to walk through the front doors of the airport.

I slowly made my way to the check-in counter and then up the escalator holding on to the rails, hoping I would not see anyone who knew me. I waited at the gate praying the entire time, asking God if I should cancel. All I could hear from God was that He had given me peace and I needed to trust Him. The call to board came, and I went, holding onto the rails going up the jetway, having difficulty keeping my balance. Praise God, I got settled in my seat! As usual, I slept on the one-hour flight from Sioux Falls to Minneapolis.

My strength had not returned when I disembarked the plane at the Minneapolis-St. Paul International Airport. I praised God for the cart that carried me to the next gate marked "AMSTERDAM." I found chairs at the gate with no armrests, and I laid down over three chairs.

I heard the boarding call and got up. I prayed that if I was not given the strength I needed by the time I was settled in my seat on the plane, I would get off and find a way home. I got about halfway up the jetway when the healing came! It happened suddenly, something like a warm wash came over me, not with water, but smooth as butter, from the top of my head down to my shoulders, all the way to my toes. It was so special, like nothing I ever felt before. It had to be the power of the Holy Spirit! I praised God, my strength was returning. I had a big smile on my face, I straightened up and walked like I was thirty years old again. Those few seconds seemed like several minutes and lasted through the time it took me to find my seat on that wide-bodied jet. God tested me and He was true to His promise when I heard Him say *trust me!* I was filled with praise to my God!

On most of my many long overseas trips, I slept soundly and was somewhat rested by the time I landed in Amsterdam. On that flight, I felt relaxed and didn't even dose. Wow, when God moved, it was real and wonderful.

I had the strength to carry out my plans in Romania and gradually gained more strength. Even today I praise God that He chose to heal me. A very small percentage of people are healed from that terrible disease, but I was one of them!

***

The dictator-run communist government of Ukraine, a part of the Soviet Union, was overthrown. God used me in a small way to influence the "establishment" of the new democracy, although I was involved for only a part of an afternoon. The time I spent with the head of the Parliament, the equivalent to our Speaker of the House, was a powerful, God-moving moment.

I had been touring the Ukrainian capital of Kyiv with a group of Americans when the Ukrainians found out that I was a former senator. They passed the information on to the head of the Parliament of Ukraine and he invited me to his office. After the dark years of Communism, that person was working on drafting a new constitution for their country. He asked if I would explain the Balance of Powers, sometimes called "checks and balances" in the U.S. Constitution.

He admitted he didn't understand that part of our Constitution. I spent time teaching him about the importance of this system. I carefully explained the work and purpose of the Legislative Branch, the Administrative Branch, and the Judicial Branch.

We also discussed the difference between the state and federal systems. He was a good listener, a great note-taker, and seemed to be a quick learner. I emphasized the importance of including the balance of power in their new constitution.

When I left his office to join my group, I stood for a moment on the steps of the Ukrainian Capitol Building and was amazed at what had just happened. Though I would never get credit for helping with the writing of the Constitution of Ukraine, I had input into this very important document that was essential in establishing their new democracy. I had been used as a tool in the hands of God as His ambassador.

While serving in Romania, God allowed me to serve along with many wonderful people. Randy Tift and Gabi Achim were key in introducing me to several members of the new Romanian Parliament after the communist government was overthrown. Romania was also in the process of forming a democracy. The old State Senate business cards I carried with me came in handy at times! The cards seemed to open the doors of the government for us. We had wonderful times helping the new members of the Romanian Parliament write and pass legislation! They were so appreciative of my work with them that they presented me with a lapel pin making me an honorary member of the Romanian Parliament; I treasure it today.

I recall what Representative George Mann, my friend from the Minnesota Legislature told me: "If you are not concerned about who gets the credit, you can get a lot done in the legislative process." I found that to be true in ministry as well. I love serving the Lord; it is so exciting and gratifying. It is much greater to know that I was carrying out the work of God than to get the credit and honor of men. Wow, God has given me many great experiences! Again, I remembered the Prayer of Jabez and how God was answering my prayer asking for the expansion of my territory.

Gabi, Randy, and I helped to establish a Bible study at the Romanian Parliament. We also had many opportunities to share the good news of Jesus with many people in Romania.

***

I traveled extensively for CRWRC by plane and by car. One day on a short flight between Sioux Falls, South Dakota, and Minneapolis, Minnesota, the lady sitting next to me began shaking and crying. This was her first flight and we hit bad weather. She admitted she was scared and not ready to die. Over the next half-hour, I opened my Bible and shared with her how to find her way to the Lord.

She prayed with me asking Jesus to come into her heart. She

accepted Him as her personal Savior, all before the plane landed. I don't remember her name, and I didn't have an opportunity to disciple her, but I believe that I will see her in heaven.

***

At about eight o'clock one morning on a return of one of my monthly trips from Pella, Iowa I was traveling a county road to our home in Rock Valley, Iowa. I was stopped by a flag lady in a construction zone. It was early morning and the road was quiet, no cars were coming from either direction.

The lady seemed distressed so I asked her if I could pray for her. That brought a flood of tears, she said she was going through hard times. We prayed right there, she holding the flag, and me sitting in my car.

Then I shared with her the old, old, story of Jesus and His love. I told her how to accept Jesus into her life and I gave her a copy of my book, *Us Four.* I also gave her my calling card, assured her that I would continue to pray for her, and asked her to call me if I could be of further help.

Later, she wrote me a beautiful letter informing me that she prayed to ask Jesus into her heart after meeting me. She said she was living for Jesus and was doing much better. I have the letter to this day.

About ten years later I went to preach in a small town in the Hawarden Christian Reformed Church in Northwest Iowa, and there she was! She thanked me for sharing the Gospel with her and said she was still excited about living for Jesus. God expects us to be His ambassadors, any place, any time.

Five

Wedding, Grandkids, and the Big Move

*For I know the plans I have for you — this is the Lord's
declaration—"plans for your well-being, not for disaster,
to give you a future and a hope."*
Jeremiah 29:11 [CSB]

Our family's Utah connection started in Mitch's junior year at Dordt
College. In March of 1994, Mitch and a couple of upperclassmen
organized and led a Putting Love Into Action (PLIA) Spring Break,
missions-work project trip to Jackson, Mississippi.

"I'm kind of finished with dating," Mitch had said. "I'm not going
to go on this trip looking for a girlfriend." Famous last words. On the
second or third night, he found himself chatting with a freshman from
Salt Lake City, Kara Van Heyst. Mitch led the evening devotions on
the trip and noticed that she was one person in the group who tended to
agree with him! After devotions one evening, sparks began to fly when
he showed her how to peel an orange with a spoon. The talk lasted late
into the night. There must have been a lot of oranges to peel.

Our son's heart began to beat harder than usual. After they returned
to college, Mitch asked her out for their first date on April Fool's Day.
Both were smitten, the match was struck, and that was the beginning of
the fire that would change not only their lives, but ours, too.

In a little over two years, Mitch and Kara were married on June 15, 1996 in Utah. The wedding was a gorgeous event and we had a wonderful time while we were there. Dawn and I hosted the rehearsal dinner at Sugarhouse Park in Salt Lake City. Many people helped, especially the Sprik family. The wedding was in a small church, nestled in a forest of trees on a mountainside, with many large windows, near Park City, Utah. The scene was spectacular, God's masterpiece prepared for such a moment. It was all so much fun and a very meaningful experience attended by many out-of-town guests.

Mitch bestowed on me one of the greatest honors of my lifetime. He asked me to be his best man. Michael was a groomsman, assisted by Kara's brother, Greg. Dawn and I walked Mitch down the aisle. On that trip, Utah started to grow on us.

Mitch and Kara moved to Chicago after their wedding. Mitch taught for a year at Timothy Christian School and Kara finished her senior year at Trinity Christian College, earning a Bachelor of Science degree in nursing.

A year later they moved to Nashville where they lived for three years. Mitch taught at Christ Presbyterian Academy. Kara worked as a nurse at Vanderbilt University Hospital and then entered a rigorous program to earn her Master of Science in nursing which led her to become a nurse practitioner. Dawn and I were blessed to be able to visit them several times in Chicago and Nashville. In 2000, after attending Kara's graduation, we helped them make their big move to Salt Lake City. Mitch left teaching and entered the accounting world.

On my birthday in 2001, on July 27, I received a small package in the mail. I opened it and couldn't believe the contents of the package. It was addressed to "Grandpa Marion Menning." It was a "positive" pregnancy test. I still have that pregnancy test, filed away, and who knows when it might show up at the most unexpected time!

In the fall of 2001, Dawn and I made a trip to Salt Lake with our motorhome. We were so excited to see Mitch, Kara, and a baby on the way. However, there was a dark cloud hanging over our time together. For several years our prayer had been and we believed that Dawn and I would one day live near our grandchildren, and watch them grow and develop. Our daughter-in-law was now pregnant, but we lived over 1,100 miles away.

As we left from Salt Lake City to our home in the Midwest, Dawn finally shared a few of her inmost thoughts. She reminded me we had prayed and prayed that perhaps one day we could live close to Mitch and Kara and our grandkids. "Now, here we are," she said, tearfully. "Kara and Mitch are expecting their first child, our first grandchild, and God has not yet answered our prayers and our heart's desire to live near our kids and grandkids."

I reminded her that I had no idea how it was going to happen, but I believed with all my heart God would answer our prayer and that one day we would live near Mitch, Kara, and our grandchildren. In my heart and mind, I knew we would be able to see our grandkids grow up. Dawn left the passenger's seat and went to the back of the RV to lie down on the bed. I knew she was crying for many miles as I drove, headed east on Interstate 80.

On Christmas Eve 2001, we finished the fun time of opening family gifts. Michael was home and Mitch and Kara were visiting us in Rock Valley. On a very cold, sub-zero temperature night in the Midwest, we had a precious time relaxing and talking in the warmth and coziness of our home. We talked about Mitch and Kara living in Salt Lake City, us in Rock Valley, and dreaming out loud about how the future might look.

I was sharing from the heart, talking about a recurring thought that came to my mind over the years. I shared with our family that perhaps someday God would call me to pastor a small church. I think it was one of those times when I was thinking out loud. Little did I know that this statement would stick in our minds!

After fifteen years of working with the CRWRC, I knew deep

down that I was nearing the point of having worked myself out of a job in Eastern Europe. It was the Holy Spirit who was beginning the process of preparing me for the future as He had done so many times before.

I had reached the goal of getting the Romanian ministry to operate on its own after five years. Some denominational leaders were talking about the possibility of me leading both the Christian Reformed World Missions and CRWRC diaconal ministry in Eastern Europe. I was also in the process of seeking ordination as an ordained evangelist which would give me license to preach in Christian Reformed Churches.

After Mitch and Kara returned to Salt Lake City, the thought of me becoming a pastor didn't leave their minds or mine. Mitch was on the search committee of their small Christian Reformed congregation. Mountain Springs Community Church (MSCC) had been without a pastor for the past five years, except for a five-month stint in 2000.

In those days it was very, very difficult to find a pastor willing to move to Utah. For Christian pastors, Utah was considered a dead-end street. According to a study done by the Salt Lake Theological Seminary, during the period from 1985 to 2000, the average length of stay for pastors serving Christian churches in Utah was only nineteen months.

A few days after they returned home, the conversations began about the potential of me serving as pastor of MSCC. On a couple of previous visits to Salt Lake, I had preached in their church. The search committee was interested in pursuing the potential of asking if we were willing to fly to Salt Lake and be interviewed for the pastor position at MSCC. I met with their search team on a group call. They asked if I would preach on that Sunday as well. We talked it over and prayed about it. It was clear, we had peace and booked the flight to Salt Lake City.

I sent the Mountain Springs worship planner the Bible passage I intended to use as the basis for Sunday's message, the final verses of the book of John, chapter 21:15-19. This is the story of the reinstatement of Peter. It tells the story of Jesus asking Peter three times, "Do you love me?" What a great story and a powerful lesson on how to serve Jesus! He used the analogy of how to care for sheep as a lesson to Peter in caring for God's people on earth because Peter was about to become a church planter.

I worked hard preparing that sermon. About ten days before we left I received a call from a member of the worship team. She explained to me that they were interviewing another pastor and he would be preaching the Sunday before I was scheduled.

I thought that was fine, however, she went on to explain that the other candidate for pastor planned to use the same passage. She asked if I was willing to choose another passage. I thought for a moment and suggested that if we both preached on the same passage it would be a pretty good way for the search committee and the congregation to compare the two messages. She agreed. I didn't tell her that I only had three sermons in my repertoire of sermons. I imagined the other guy might have several hundred in his files!

We flew to Salt Lake and interviewed with the search committee. I preached the sermon. The story is so exciting when Jesus teaches how to care for "sheep." Being raised on the farm, I certainly had an advantage over the other fellow. My excitement for the story shone through. The congregation voted and asked me to serve as their next pastor.

We prayed earnestly and considered the new calling in our lives. For many years when making big decisions in my life I claimed the passage found in John 14:27, "Peace I leave with you; my peace I give you. I do not give to you as the world gives. Do not let your hearts be troubled and do not be afraid." [NIV]

We received peace from God as described in that verse. I accepted the call from MSCC and the divine call from God. I knew the position would be a reduction in salary and benefits. Once again I changed my career. At age 57, I became a pastor. I took off the "golden handcuffs" of serving as a denominational employee with a good income. However, God answered our prayers in the affirmative, and a great joy was that we would live in the same area as Mitch and Kara and their children.

The second match was struck, a small flame on the end of a match that turned into an enormous fire leading us on a journey God prepared. This fire changes our lives until Christ returns or we are called to our eternal home.

On April 15, 2002, exactly fifteen years to the day that I started my work with CRWRC, with a lump in my throat, I submitted my resignation from a job I thoroughly enjoyed.

I had mixed emotions but I was looking forward to my new calling in the ministry! After living in a small town in the Midwest all our lives, we were moving to a city to start an entirely new way of life, something we had never experienced before. On Saturday, July 6, 2002, all our earthly possessions loaded in two U-Haul trucks, our car, our van, and a small trailer, arrived at our newly purchased home in Salt Lake City.

We also moved Michael from Hope Haven – all because God called us to a new place in his world. Moving Michael from a Christ-centered agency to a state where there was no such thing caused us to lean on God in every way. As painful as it was for us to move Michael, we knew it was God's plan for our lives.

"For I know the plans I have for you — this is the LORD's declaration — plans for your well-being, not for disaster, to give you a future and a hope." Jeremiah 29:11 [CSB] We clung tightly to the promises!

Reflections & Pondering
Section 2

Chapters 4-5

So we are Christ's ambassadors; God is making his appeal
through us. We speak for Christ when we plead,
"Come back to God."
2 Corinthians 5:20 [NLT]

Reflections on <u>Your</u> Life

In Chapter 5 Mike talks about "trip theology." He mentions God speaking to Abraham, Joseph, King David, and others while they were on trips. These great people of God heard the voice of God through words, whispers, and other means. Read Jeremiah 29:11 again.

While traveling across Minnesota God spoke to Mike about running for governor. In Chapter 3 as he brought his son Michael back to the group home God gave Mike peace in his heart to move to Rock Valley. While on a ministry trip with Joni and Friends, chapter 4 tells of how God touched Mike's heart, encouraging him to start a ministry in Romania. While in Gjakova, Kosovo, God urged Mike to go to Washington to design legislation negotiating the release of the Gjakova 81 prisoners of war. Mike tells of a time he led a lady to the Lord on a flight to Minneapolis. He tells about how his son Mitch met his future wife on a mission trip. A few years later, after a Christmas visit to his parents, Mitch asks them to consider moving to Salt Lake City to pastor their church.

Do you think "trip theology" is a suitable phrase for how God often speaks to his people? In light of biblical history, God spoke to people while on a trip or away from home. How does this " trip theology" apply to you, and have you experienced God putting something on your heart, or speaking to you while on a trip?

Do you think Pete Boer, a good farmer, truck driver, and deacon in his church, saw himself as an ambassador of Jesus when he recommended Mike for the Diaconal Consultant position with the Christian Reformed Church denomination? How did Pete demonstrate his ambassadorship?

Do you have any other thoughts about God using small beginnings according to Zechariah 4:10a?

Mike still considers himself a farm kid from Minnesota. He says that he was simply, "a tool in the hand of God," concerning Congress passing legislation resulting in the release of Gjakova, Kosovo 81 prisoners of war. What do you think he meant by that statement?

Do you have any thoughts going through your mind concerning Mike's miraculous healing from Chronic Fatigue Syndrome? How does a story like this affect you?

In chapter 5 we learn of God calling the Mennings to move to Utah with all its challenges. What are the challenges you are facing in your life? How can you deal with them?

Do you have other questions, comments, or thoughts concerning the stories in Chapters 4 or 5?

Give this some thought. Can you see yourself maturing as an *ambassador of Jesus* by following God's lead and being sensitive to His communication, no matter how great or small?

Pondering <u>Your</u> Life's Direction

Did anything in chapters 4 and 5 cause you to consider making a **Heart Change** within your life? If so, what part or story caught your attention?

Are there **Life Changes** you need to make to mature as an *ambassador of Jesus*?

Section Three

New Ministries

Six

Mountain Springs Community Church

*What no eye has seen, nor ear heard, nor the heart of man
imagined, what God has prepared for those who love him.*
2 Corinthians 2:9 [ESV]

In July 2002, a crowd of over twenty people, our new church family,
awaited us when we arrived with two U-Haul trucks at our new
home. They got our belongings moved into our thirty-year-old home
in Cottonwood Heights, Utah. Our home was a half-mile from the
church. I liked that since most of the year I walked to work, home for
lunch, back for the afternoon, and then home again.

I was 57 years old and starting a whole new career. As soon as
we got somewhat settled I was off to the office to start my new work.
For the past fifteen years, I had spent much of my time working with
pastors and church leaders. However, being a pastor was a whole new
story, I knew God called me to be a pastor.

I didn't have to prepare a sermon until the second Sunday after
we arrived. That was good because I had to organize my office and get
to know the church council and the volunteers on the worship planning
team. They were great people and very helpful.

Serving as pastor in the Mountain Springs Community Church

(MSCC) had many blessings. To this day I am thankful for the wonderful experiences, although the work had some pretty big challenges. The people were wonderful and I praise God for the opportunity to have served Him there.

Because I had been a fifteen-year employee of the Christian Reformed Church denomination, I had a good understanding of the culture and operation of the church. The denomination was known for operating in an orderly fashion. It has been said that for some in the CRC, orderliness was next to godliness.

I knew I was where God wanted me to be in my new position as the pastor of MSCC. Because I had not been theologically trained at the denomination's seminary, leaders of the denomination required me to be examined theologically before I could be ordained.

I was to be publicly examined by an ordained pastor from Classis Yellowstone, the regional governing classis of the Christian Reformed Church. The entire process was overseen by Synodical Deputies, three pastors from different parts of the country. One of the pastors was from the East Coast, one from the West Coast, and one from the Midwest. These men were to observe the examination process, making sure that everything was done in an orderly fashion, making sure the t's were crossed and the i's were dotted. This was all following the denominational rules and regulations, and everything was done according to the Christian Reformed Church Order.

When the day of my classical exam came, I felt like I was ready to face the team of examiners. In my fifteen years of work as a denominational employee, I attended many regional meetings of candidates who were examined as they journeyed the path toward ordination in the CRC.

I was asked to sit up front and face the examiners, the onlookers, friends, and family who gathered. It was a tough exam, especially in the presence of all those folks with great denominational influence. At the conclusion of the examination, I was asked to leave the room while the examiners met. There were a few concerns, but in the end, I was ordained as a "Pastor" in the Christian Reformed Church.

God blessed our ministry at MSCC. My work flourished and I believe God was blessed. In the five years I served as pastor of that little church, I officiated a total of 46 baptisms, 11 infants and 35 adults, many of these had been raised in the Mormon religion.

Our son Michael was also blessed at MSCC. Michael had friends there as well and loved it. Many times he sat with Simon VanBeek, an older man from the congregation, who became Michael's friend. Sometimes Michael and he sat together in the back of the auditorium.

Following God's will for our lives is not an easy task. For Michael the move was not a cakewalk either, he paid a price for relocating. So often in society, we forget or never know how people with developmental disabilities are affected. Even people like Michael, who can't express themselves, go through hard times. About six months after our big move to Utah we saw that Michael was seriously impacted because he began showing signs of depression.

In a miraculous way during that same time, God showed us what was happening in Michael's life. Dawn and I attended a farewell party for a family of our church where we met a young man. We introduced ourselves. The fellow asked if we were related to Michael Menning. We were excited to hear that he had been one of Michael's care workers. He explained that he was working on his master's degree at the University of Utah and had done an internship with the group home where Michael was living. While we sat to eat our lunch, he came back to us and said, "I need to talk with you guys!"

He seemed a little shaken but explained that we needed to know about things that were going on at the group home. He told us that he and several others had been fired because they didn't go along with the social life at the group home. He said that the internal management of the group home was gay and that after the clients were put to bed there were times the staff had sexual orgies. Those of the staff who opposed these actions were let go. The man then gave us a parting comment – perhaps God put Michael in that place for the sake of the other clients. I reported those findings to the state and later we were informed that the majority of the staff at that group home were fired. It was several months before we were able to find another placement for Michael, but things changed drastically in the facility and the staff.

In the fall we found another group home for Michael. It was thirty minutes north of us and seemed much better for him. He was happy and well cared for. We began to understand that we, like in the book of Esther, were placed in Utah for "such a time as this."

***

On our third day in Utah, July 8, 2002, Dawn and I went to the local Walmart. It was there that I met Bill Wingeier. While standing in line to order a bite to eat at the snack bar, I suddenly heard this deep voice behind me, saying, "So, ya' planning on doing ministry in Utah?"

I was quite shocked, to say the least. I turned around and standing there behind me was an older giant of a man. I think he stood at least 6 feet 5 inches. "Yeah, how did you know?" I responded.

"Don't you know what the h--- you are wearing?"

I was wearing a t-shirt and on the back was printed, "Justice For All Ministries, Rock Valley, Iowa." It turned out Bill was very familiar with Northwest Iowa from his truck driving days. I asked Bill to join me for a bite to eat at a nearby table.

We soon discovered that both of us had diabetes and needed to eat to satisfy our low blood sugar. We started sharing about health issues and I realized his health was not good. He was a bold man. *If you can be so bold, so can I*, I thought. I said to my new friend, "Considering all your health issues, it sounds like you could die anytime. If you were to die tonight, are you ready, where would you go?"

Suddenly Bill stopped cursing. "We need to talk."

I met Bill for coffee at Walmart weekly for the next few months. On the Sunday before Thanksgiving, Bill and his wife, Caroline, met Dawn at the entrance to our church. At the door, he said to Dawn, "This is the first time I stepped my foot across the threshold of a church in 52 years."

Two months later, in January 2003, I had the privilege of baptizing Bill and Caroline. Oh, how I came to love this big guy and his family. I could write a book on my adventures with "Big Bill." I was with him when he died and officiated his memorial service. Although Bill's character was rough at times, he was a good man in many ways. I look forward to him greeting me when I too arrive in paradise.

***

A friend of mine, Steve Shogren, attended the Mountain Springs Community Church. He had a buddy from high school named Jim. Jim grew up in Utah and Steve in Idaho. Years before they were master trumpet players who had been chosen to play in an elite high school traveling band. They hadn't seen each other for many, many years but in their mid-fifties, Steve and Jim met again in Utah.

Steve invited Jim to visit our church. On a few occasions, they played their trumpets for our worship service. I got to know Jim and soon found out he had never given his life to Jesus.

Jim and I met for breakfast every month for two years. I took him through the "Romans Road" verses from the Bible. I walked him through the "Bill Faye" presentation for salvation. I prayed regularly for Jim.

Jim had many problems. He got off drugs and alcohol, but not before his wife, whom he loved very much, left him. He didn't completely lose his children, but the relationship was strained. At one time he had a very prestigious job as Fire Chief of the Park City, Utah

Fire Department, but more recently he was working as an hourly wage earner for the Red Cross.

I walked life with Jim and he attended church regularly. Two years passed and Jim never felt he was ready to pray to receive Christ into his life, but I never gave up on him.

One day Jim and I were having coffee together and he shared from the heart. "Mike, I appreciate the fact that you have never given up on me, but there is something I need to tell you. I enjoy coming to church and being your friend, but you need to understand that I cannot commit to accepting the Lord until I feel it in my heart." Pointing to his head, he went on, "I have it up here, but it hasn't traveled down here (pointing to his heart). When that happens, I'll be ready and I'll let you know."

Time passed and I continued meeting with Jim and our friendship matured. About ten minutes before our worship service was to start on August 14, 2005, I was standing beside the piano in the front of the auditorium, and out of the corner of my eye, I saw Jim coming down the east side aisle of the church. He called out to me with the biggest smile on his face. "Mike, Mike, come here."

I greeted him, and he gave me a big bear hug. "Mike, I did it during the night."

"Jim, you did what?"

"I got on my knees beside the bed, confessed my sins, and asked Jesus into my heart."

Jim explained that during the night God had awakened him and "dealt with him." He remembered much of what we had talked about. And then, Jim got down on his knees, alone in that apartment, and did what he told me he would do at the right moment. The Holy Spirit worked on Jim in the Lord's timing, I rejoiced with him and celebrated with the angels in heaven. Luke 15:10 says, "In the same way, I tell you, there is rejoicing in the presence of the angels of God over one sinner who repents." [NIV]

Jim and I practiced what I called "restaurant theology." We often had breakfast at Denny's. I have discipled and led many people to Christ in restaurants. Hence the term "restaurant theology!" I encouraged Jim to be baptized the next Sunday and he agreed wholeheartedly. Jim was baptized on August 21. His former wife whom he had never forgotten and a couple of his children came for the celebration of his baptism. Jim was a new man and able to face the challenges of life in a new way. Our friendship continued.

A year later on the very date of his baptism, Jim and Steve were scheduled to play their trumpets in the morning worship service. On these occasions, Steve and Jim would get to church early to practice. That Sunday morning Jim didn't show up, which was unusual. Steve told me later he just figured that perhaps Jim was not feeling well and stayed in bed.

After the service, Steve was concerned and went to Jim's apartment. He rang the bell and knocked on the door. There was no answer. Steve went to the manager's office and finally convinced the manager to come with him and unlock the door.

Steve discovered that his friend of more than thirty years had died in his bed. Jim passed away on August 21, 2006, exactly one year from the date of his baptism. Five days later Steve's wife Cindy, an ordained pastor in the Presbyterian Church, and I officiated Jim's funeral at Mt. Olympus Presbyterian Church. Since Jim was a former Park City Fire Chief, he was given a fireman's funeral, this was all new to me! The service was somewhat similar to a military funeral. Jim was to be buried in the Park City Cemetery. As we left the church parking lot in Salt Lake City, the funeral procession was led by two fire engines in the front, then the coach, followed by the family, and then Pastor Cindy, her husband Steve, and me. Behind us was another fire engine. To our surprise, as we headed toward the Park City Cemetery, at each entrance onto Interstate 80 more fire trucks joined the procession. I am guessing that by the time we arrived at the cemetery, there were perhaps a total of 15 to 20 firetrucks escorting the funeral procession. Before we did the graveside service, there was the fireman's service. This consisted of a few words from the fire chief at the time and then they rang a bell which was mounted on a 1930s fire truck. The gong hit the bell many times, which is a tradition for a fireman's funeral. It was a beautiful graveside service, but nothing like the welcome Jim received when he arrived at his heavenly home, when the angels, in the presence of God, welcomed him home!

***

The scam caller thought he was going to get me, but in the end, the Lord got him. I had advertised our Chrysler Town and Country van for sale and a Nigerian guy who claimed he worked on an offshore oil well drilling platform responded to my ad via text.

The offer he made was too good to be true, and when that is the case I find that most of the time it is too good to be true. I asked him to call me back, I wanted to get his personal phone number; and I did. I said I had a better deal for him than he had with the people he was working for.

After the ice was broken we had a good conversation. He told me he needed work for the unscrupulous company making the scam calls because of the needs of his wife, children, and aging parents. I told him about Jesus and His promises.

Tears followed, and after an hour of conversation, I led him to Jesus on the phone. I told this guy that I would continue praying to ask God to help him find a better job.

I called my friend, Dr. Gary Bekker, Director of Christian Reformed World Missions, and told him the story. I asked if he would connect the scam caller who accepted Jesus with a local Christian pastor of a church in his home city in Nigeria. Gary made contact and a Nigerian Christian pastor met the guy and agreed to disciple him. I'll repeat it; God works in mysterious ways, even through something as annoying as a scam call. In time I learned to share Jesus with many of the scam callers who contact me.

***

Late one evening about five years after I began my position as pastor, I was walking home after a council meeting. It was dark and I was reviewing one of the discussions at the meeting. I felt the Lord was telling me that my time of pastoring MSCC was coming to a close. This message from God was as clear as the morning He called me out of the political world.

But I wrestled with God. I didn't anticipate leaving the pastorate only five years after starting this new endeavor. I pleaded with Him to give me peace about staying at the church. When I first arrived at the MSCC we had an attendance of about 30 to 35 people on Sunday morning. I remember one Sunday morning, shortly after we arrived in Utah (I think it was over a holiday weekend) we had about fifteen people in attendance. As time passed, little by little, we grew. Near the end of my ministry, we had an average Sunday morning attendance of about 100.

Several days later I vividly remember walking from the little gray office building toward the church. I passed the garbage dumpster and cried out to the Lord, *God, don't you understand that if you are calling me into another ministry. Something new again? How am I to care for our family? You do realize, don't you, that I have diabetes, and taking care of that will cost me over $900 a month?*

All I heard from God was, *I called Abraham to go and he didn't know where he was going. I am calling you to trust me. Just trust me!*

Okay, God, you win.

A couple of weeks later I announced to the congregation that I would be leaving, even though I did not know where God was taking me. But, I did know He was calling me away from serving as pastor of MSCC. I knew God was, once again, testing me, and I wasn't happy. The new vision He gave me was for a ministry with no financial benefits or guaranteed salary.

After I preached my farewell sermon, a member of the council informed me that they decided to grant us a severance package. I had not asked for it, but they said they would continue my salary for six months and would continue my health insurance for a full year. God takes care of us when we follow Him!

It was a great time for me. During my tenure with MSCC, I felt God leading and molding me to become a more mature ambassador of the King.

Seven

Pastor to Pastors -
Ministry with Polygamy Culture

*Then Jesus came to them and said, "All authority in heaven
and on earth has been given to me. Therefore go and make disciples
of all nations, baptizing them in the name of the Father
and of the Son and of the Holy Spirit, and teaching
them to obey everything I have commanded you.
And surely I am with you always, to the very end of the age."*
Matthew 28: 18-20 [NIV]

*Like an open book, you watched me grow from conception to birth;
all the stages of my life were spread out before you. The days of my
life all prepared before I'd even lived one day.*
Psalm 139:16 [The Message]

At age sixty-two, I was seeking God's guidance for direction about
where he would lead me next. After all, I knew God had a plan for
all of us. But, that plan wasn't clear and I continued to struggle. Would
the new direction be a great challenge or would God have someone
give me a call as he did twenty years earlier when I went to work for
CRWRC? Time passed and God began to show me a vision of what
was needed for Christian pastors in Utah.

Many people familiar with the State of Utah have felt a dark spiritual cloud hanging over it. I remembered my former boss sharing some of his insights with me when I informed him that I was leaving CRWRC, moving to Utah, and pastoring a church in Salt Lake City. He told me that he was happy for me and knew me well enough to know that it was God leading me, but he said he would not plan to visit me in Utah. I was somewhat taken aback. He explained that when he had been in Salt Lake on a few occasions, he felt spiritual darkness to the point of being very uncomfortable.

Knowing this and the realities I had experienced as a pastor in Utah, God led me into a ministry of being a pastor to pastors and church planters. Many pastors were leaving Utah and almost all of them talked about how their wives were very lonely and their families were experiencing demonic attacks.

I believe Satan and his forces attack ministry leaders in different ways, in different geographical areas. Here in Utah, the attacks would often happen in dreams at night. The dreams might occur as often as three or four nights a week. I had not experienced this until I moved to Utah. In our family it hit me, and I am grateful that it only rarely affected Dawn. We don't believe Michael was affected by it, and for that we praise God; however, we don't know for sure, as Michael can't tell us.

Years before, I had seen this same kind of spiritual warfare in places like Kenya and Romania. At one point, I asked a former missionary friend of mine who had worked in Africa, to come to do a workshop on how our church planters and pastors could do spiritual warfare and restrain Satan. The workshop was well attended. The advice was quite simple and something I had already practiced for several years. When I was being attacked in a demonic dream, I woke up, got out of bed, went to the living room, got on my knees, and, in the name of Jesus, ordered the demons to leave. Sometimes it didn't happen immediately, it might take a few minutes. I could feel it when it was over since I no longer felt their presence. Then I was able to go back to bed and sleep peacefully.

I knew I had to do something that I didn't relish, but God placed in my heart the need to humble myself, get out there, and raise the money needed to establish the ministry. But, first I needed to spend much time in prayer. We called the new ministry Pastor to Pastors.

I started contacting churches in the Midwest as well as pastors I knew and those who knew me. Then I called many of my friends and acquaintances, explaining to them where God was leading me. The response was very positive. God had prepared their hearts ahead of my phone calls. Support for the new ministry gained momentum and I was able to start the new ministry.

The pastors in Utah were very appreciative and many shared the struggles they were going through. Some began calling other pastors who wanted to get together. I soon found myself up to my eyeballs in the new ministry working with and encouraging pastors.

God led me into two areas of ministry. I served as a pastor to pastors of established churches as well as to many of the church planters across the state. Many pastors, Utah church planters, and their families were hurting.

Some church planters came to Utah with little prayer and financial support. Some came with good intentions and "parachuted in," which means they did not have supporting churches and were not "sent" by mission organizations or from a home church. Many found themselves very lonely with little understanding of the local culture, and the people they were trying to reach. Though I did the best I could, there was no way I could counsel, mentor, or help all of them.

Instead, I was led to another model. I got many of the church planters to meet together in geographical areas about every two weeks. As much as I was able, I attempted to get pastors of established churches to meet with the church planters about every three months. They shared, prayed, laughed, and cried together; becoming trusted friends and brothers in Christ. This networking helped them immensely.

For many, the Utah mission field is a difficult place for Christian pastors to raise their families. There are many Utah communities with 95% to 98% of the population who are Mormon. In some Mormon communities, parents do not allow their children to play with the children of pastors. This attitude varied by community. The kids who suffered the most were eight-year-old Christian children who attended public schools. Mormon children are usually baptized at age eight, and they are excited to talk about it. This put a lot of pressure on the Christian missionary kids to be baptized as well. As a result, many of the children of pastors were homeschooled.

It's not surprising that many church planters left after six months to a year. I said if they could make it through two years, the chances of surviving or thriving in Utah were pretty good. Still, with some encouragement and mentoring, many new Christian churches were established and grew. I loved strengthening young pastors and my work was flourishing.

***

Only a few months after we arrived in Utah, God placed Danielle, a wonderful young single mom, into our lives. She and her five children left her polygamist husband. Our daughter-in-law, Kara, a Nurse Practitioner, worked at a neurology clinic, and she got to know Danielle at the clinic. Danielle was diagnosed with multiple sclerosis. Kara wasn't able to tell us about Danielle but mentioned to Danielle that perhaps her father-in-law might be able to help her. Kara gave Danielle my phone number, and she contacted me. Immediately Dawn and I went to visit her and her children. More visits followed, including some with her special friend, Rene, from El Salvador.

We invited Danielle, Rene, and her five children for Thanksgiving dinner in 2002. God put this wonderful family into the hearts of our family. Eventually, the entire family accepted Jesus. That spring I had the privilege of officiating the marriage of Danielle and Rene. He became a wonderful husband and father to her children. We met more of her family. Some of her siblings continued the practice of plural marriage.

In 2006 our church, MSCC, and K2 the Church built this family a large new home, all with volunteers and much donated materials.

During the time of the building of the house, Rene, Danielle's husband came to me and asked for our blessing on taking Danielle to a church in his home country of El Salvador. That church practiced the ministry of "healing." At first, I was not very encouraged, but then through prayer, the Lord made it very clear to me that they should go. Wow, that church prayed over Danielle, for about four days, sometimes many hours a day. Danielle came home healed of her MS.

Later Dawn and I went to El Salvador to observe what we referred to as the "healing church." Wow, what a great gathering of dedicated people, some of whom God had given the gift of healing.

Their family of eight lived with us in our home for almost a year! Many of the blessings of that experience were ours.

The story of Danielle doesn't stop there. Danielle and her family experienced blessings beyond imagination. God provided them with a spacious new home and she was miraculously healed from multiple sclerosis.

Even though her father and mother took her out of school in the seventh grade, later in life, this mother of seven was able to earn her high school diploma. She went on to earn a college degree and taught Spanish in a Christian school for many years. During that time she also earned a master's degree. God gave Rene and her a vibrant prayer ministry. She has a very bright mind and much wisdom. She and her family have faced many trials.

Because of our acquaintance with Danielle, God prepared us to begin to understand the polygamist culture. At that time, the news was coming out about Warren Jeffs, the prophet of the polygamist group, the Fundamentalist Latter Day Saints (FLDS). They, like the mainline Mormon church, followed the teachings of Joseph Smith. One of the differences between these two groups is that the mainline Mormon church does not condone the practice of polygamy here on earth, but they do believe in polygamy in the next life.

The issue of polygamy started to receive national attention around the turn of the century. Jeffs, the prophet of the FLDS ruled the people of his cult with an iron fist. They were called to live in the twin towns of Colorado City, Arizona, and Hildale, Utah (CC/H, also known as "Short Creek" or "The Crick") before 2000. Jeffs was on the FBI's "Ten Most Wanted" list. He was arrested in 2006, and convicted to a life sentence, plus twenty years for performing an underage marriage and taking a twelve-year-old as one of his many wives. He is serving his prison sentence in Texas and yet he rules from his prison cell to this day.

On the Saturday after Thanksgiving 2011, Dawn and I were leaving St. George, Utah in the southern part of the state, after spending the evening with Joel and Izabella, one of our "Romanian daughters," and their new baby boy. We were heading home when I received a phone call that changed our lives.

Tonia Tewell, Founder of Holding Out Help, an outreach ministry to people leaving the FLDS with whom we partnered closely, expected that I was in Salt Lake. She asked if I would head for CC/H to pick up a young man who needed to get out of that town by nightfall.

"You won't believe this," I told her, "we are only about thirty miles from CC/H right now."

She was so grateful. Of course, we were more than happy to help. We were excited to see the polygamist town we had heard and read so much about.

We pulled into The Crick just before dusk. We were shocked by what we saw. It was the most unkempt town I had ever seen and mentally took us back to the 1950s. Many of the streets were dirt paths.

We saw few lawns and a lot of tumbleweeds. Many of the houses were surrounded by abandoned cars, trucks, abundant piles of trash, and weeds 2-3 feet tall! Almost all the houses had six to ten-foot walls around them made of every type of material imaginable. The place was eerie.

After some searching, we finally found the address where the young man was waiting for us. Will came out of the house with four large, black garbage bags filled with all his earthly possessions. He was, about nineteen years old, a tall guy with a dark complexion. Three of his sisters came out of the house to bid him farewell. They were dressed in long prairie dresses. Their hairdos were unlike any we had ever seen. Their hair on top was combed back with a big puff in the front. Somehow, it all came together into a braid down their backs. One sister's braid went all the way down to her waist. The girls seemed to be fascinated with "people from the outside" and we were captivated by their appearance as well.

At the time, I didn't realize that many of the people and their descendants caught up in this cult had never seen a television, heard a radio, read a newspaper, or never talked with anyone from the outside. They lived in seclusion! They were so sheltered, it was like entering a time warp.

We felt a strong sense of concern. Seeds of love were planted for these folks who were victims of the evil, Mormon-based FLDS, and demonic powers that kept them from the outside world. Will seemed anxious, and we knew he had to get out of town quickly for fear that the god squad, the church's security force, might follow and force him to return. The security force drove high-riding new black Ford trucks with heavily darkened tinted windows. They followed any unfamiliar vehicles in the towns. He was also aware that the FLDS church had over 100 cameras mounted throughout the community; he knew they were capable of stopping us and could create trouble at any moment.

We tossed the garbage bags in the back of my red '99 GMC

pickup. Will commented about my red truck. Much later, after several trips into the polygamist community, I better understood his concern about me driving the "red" truck - more about that later.

My truck had a club cab, meaning a small backseat. It didn't seem to matter to Will, even though he was over six feet tall. He wanted to get out of town as quickly as possible. I felt the urgency of the situation and headed toward Hurricane, Utah.

Will had no problems talking on the 300-mile trip to Draper, Utah. He had so much to tell and so many questions. There was one remark that took Dawn and me by surprise and penetrated our hearts.

"Every year, about this time, somewhere between now and the new year, some of us who get out of town have seen this celebration of lights," he said.

What did he mean by a celebration of lights?

"People have colorful lights on their houses, fences, trees, and some even blink on and off," he explained. It dawned on us. He was talking about Christmas lights! We tried to explain that it was a way of celebrating Christmas.

"What is Christmas anyway?" he asked. We were dumbfounded.

He was 19 years old, living in the United States and he had never experienced Christmas! He had no idea that it was the celebration of Jesus' birth more than 2,000 years ago. He said they celebrated the birth of Jesus on April 6, a somewhat common belief in some Mormon circles.

We pulled over for dinner at a restaurant in a small town along Interstate 15. We sat in a booth near the window and explained the meaning of Christmas to 19-year-old Will.

God began to work on my heart at that moment. God helped me to understand the need for someone to bring the Jesus of the Bible to this "unreached people group," and that someone was me. Questions whirled through my mind for the rest of the trip home.

Arrangements were made in advance for Will to join two of his sisters living with a family in Draper, about twenty miles south of our home. It was exciting to see the siblings reunite. The two young ladies had left the FLDS about six months before. All three of them realized they were finally free from the oppression of the demonic cult.

Dawn and I arrived home late that night. The next day was Sunday. I enjoyed a good time with my family, but my mind was preoccupied with the thoughts of so many FLDS living in deep darkness. In missionary terms, this was truly an "unreached people group".

In times like these, the Spirit makes me somewhat uneasy in my daily work. It is all part of the process as I seek God's will for my life. I prayed, *Yes, Lord I will do what You want me to do, I will go where You want me to go. I am okay with Your leading, not knowing where I am headed, as long as I keep my eyes on You.* When I keep my eyes on God I find the peace of John 14:27. That is when I find joy in my work and He blesses me in ways I hadn't considered.

God spoke to me clearly, I knew that after five years I needed to begin to turn the ministry of Pastor to Pastors over to someone else. I felt I ought to start a new ministry helping people who lived in the polygamist culture. God showed me that I needed to move on.

I knew I could not just drop the remarkable ministry of Pastor to Pastors. A thought came to mind as I was praying one day. Dave Elshaug, the Director of the Children's Ministry at our church, had mentioned to me on several occasions that he wanted to make a trip with me to the community of Colorado City/Hildale. Dave told me that he felt God was leading him into different ministry. We set a date for my next trip down south. He was all in and I was excited. I smiled to myself because I knew I would have him in the truck for four and a half hours on the way down and four and a half hours on the way back. Dave would not be able to escape my challenge to take over the reins of Pastor to Pastors.

On the return trip, I explained that I thought it was time to gather a group of pastors from established churches in the Salt Lake Valley to talk about the future of Pastor to Pastors. From that group, some would be asked to serve on the board of the reorganized Pastor to Pastors ministry, and hopefully, Dave would become the new director. I knew that the ministry needed to move to a higher level. We would share with the pastors that God was leading us to a vision where established churches would care for and nourish new church plants and their leaders.

Dave and I agreed to bathe our conversation in prayer, asking God to lead and confirm what we had talked about. The Lord was definitely leading. Before long we were able to gather some area pastors and explain where God was leading us. We found that God was working ahead of us. The pastors agreed to take over and reorganize the Pastor to Pastors ministry. The newly established group asked me to serve on the Board of Directors and help make the changes needed. The new board hired Dave as the Executive Director and we renamed the ministry Loving Utah.

On February 21, 2013, I passed the baton of Pastor to Pastors to Dave at a celebration gathering of fifty-four people, mostly pastors and a few spouses. They prayed over me asking God to bless my new ministry which we had decided to name Great Commission Utah. They prayed over Dave Elshaug asking God to bless him in his role as Executive Director of Loving Utah.

Soon, I was fully engaged in the new ministry, Great Commission Utah. My goal was to reach people for Christ who were from the polygamy culture. My very good friend, Dave Roberts, reminded me that God has given me the apostolic gift of starting ministries. To clarify, I don't claim to be an apostle, but I believe God gave me a spiritual gift to start ministries and then pass them on to others, with the faith that I would see them grow to higher levels.

Eight

Great Commission Utah/Sharing Jesus

Then he said to his disciples, "The harvest is plentiful,
but the laborers are few; therefore pray earnestly to the Lord
of the harvest to send out laborers into his harvest."
Matthew 9:37-38 [ESV]

The organization of Holding Out Help contacted me to ask if I could make a few more trips to the Crick and I agreed. The Crick was 320 miles south of where we lived. Over the next few months, I made several trips there, and each time I went, I made contact with a few more of the locals.

I shared with the friends of our ministry the excitement of what I was seeing and doing, and all that God was doing. Many people were praying for me as I asked for God's guidance.

The nearly five hours of driving time each way was time well spent. Those hours were wonderful times to pray and think about how to work out God's call on my life.

I saw the first part of the vision for Great Commission Utah very clearly. The bottom line was for me to become the heart and hands of Jesus to the people of the polygamist community. Of course, the ultimate goal was to reach this unreached people group for the Jesus of the Bible.

Let me explain what I mean by "the Jesus of the Bible." Whether we are talking mainline Mormonism, Fundamentalist Mormonism (FLDS), or one of what some say are over 50 other break-offs of Mormonism, they all have a couple of beliefs in common. First of all, they are all followers of Joseph Smith. Their beliefs are primarily based on the teachings of The Book of Mormon. The Mormon King James version of the Bible is different from the Christian King James Bible, in fact, it contains about 12,000 more words than the 1611 King James version. Therefore, Christians teach the Jesus of the Christian Bible. The Mormons' Jesus is considered to be one of many sons of God, even Lucifer is considered one of Jesus' fallen brothers. There are many books written on these teachings.

The second part of the vision or purpose of the new ministry wouldn't be clear until a few years later. I planned to minister to those who had left the polygamist culture and were wandering like lost sheep without a shepherd. I was reminded of Matthew 9:35-38 "And Jesus went throughout all the cities and villages, teaching in their synagogues and proclaiming the gospel of the kingdom and healing every disease and every affliction. When he saw the crowds, he had compassion for them, because they were harassed and helpless, like sheep without a shepherd. Then he said to his disciples, "The harvest is plentiful, but the laborers are few; therefore pray earnestly to the Lord of the harvest to send out laborers into his harvest." [ESV]

We were ready to move ahead with our new mission of carrying out "The Great Commission." I needed to remind myself of that every day, so I set the alarm on my iPhone to ring at 9:38 a.m. every morning. Dawn set her phone to ring at 9:38 p.m. every evening. I asked others in my weekly newsletter, the Monday Message, to join us. I knew many across the nation used this reminder to pray daily.

I hoped to work with the three main polygamous groups in Utah, the FLDS mostly from CC/H, the First Ward in Centennial Park, and the Apostolic United Brethren, scattered throughout Idaho, Utah, and

Montana; better known as the Allreds. The Kingston clan, another large group, is scattered across Utah and Colorado.

I knew the best place to start was on my knees asking God to lead me. Psalm 119:133 says, "Direct my footsteps according to your word." [NIV]

I began by going back to take a good look around in CC/H, where God had led us in the first place. I had to communicate carefully with those who supported our ministry because we depended on the gifts of God's people and offerings from churches for prayer and financial support. Praise God, the support continued, not only in finances but also in prayer support, which was even more important. If we remained in the will of God, I knew He would not only lead, but also provide the finances needed to sustain the ministry. God provided for our needs, but not without testing us.

For many years of my life, I had the responsibility of fundraising in my campaigns for public office. I raised the money needed to do ministry while I worked for Christian Reformed World Relief. I felt I was pretty good at raising funds. However, when I founded Great Commission Utah at age sixty-seven, something changed; God was no longer blessing my efforts to raise money as He had in the past.

In 2011, the first year of this new ministry, not all the funds came in to pay my salary. I struggled with the Lord in prayer about the shortfall. I knew I was where God wanted me to be, right smack-dab in the center of his will for my life. God had always supplied our needs in the past, however, in that year of this ministry, we went for two months without a paycheck. During the second year, we went for three months without a paycheck. What was God trying to tell us? I prayed and prayed, but found no answers.

While on my knees pleading with God in December of the second year, I waited for an answer. Finally, it came as clear as though I heard an audible voice from God. I heard His kind and gentle message: *You don't have to fear, I am with you. Don't ask people for the money needed*

– trust me. Only make the needs known, and pray for the support to come. When you pray I will touch the hearts of people to support the ministry. Do not be afraid.

I took God at his word. I made the need known, Dawn and I prayed and prayed. Before long the money began to come, enough to pay the bills and my expenses, and even enough to pay me my small salary. Since we were on Social Security by then, we requested that the amount paid by the ministry be reduced.

Praise God, by the end of the third year, enough money came in to pay all my salary for that year plus the salary I had missed for the past two years! At first, this new way of following God was difficult because it was hard *not* to ask Him for funding. But oh my, there is much less stress doing it God's way. "Trust in the Lord with all your heart and lean not on your own understanding; in all your ways submit to him, and he will direct our paths." Proverbs 3:5-6 [NKJ]

***

While visiting Colorado City, Arizona, and Hildale, Utah, or "The Crick," as it was called by the locals, I often had breakfast at the Merry Wives Cafe. I met some of the locals there, those who had left the FLDS or were expelled. It took a while before I gained the trust of the local folks. I also observed an interesting small-town custom that was similar to other small towns; the gathering of the round table regulars. I joined their discussions, but there was no doubt that they kept an eye on me.

In those early years of going to The Crick, I also got to know some of the investigators who were gathering evidence about Warren Jeffs, the FLDS Prophet, as well as other leaders of the FLDS.

Jim Wylder was a long-time investigator for the County Attorney's Office. Jim was a little skeptical of me at first, but later became a good friend. The federal government also continued the FBI investigation.

I did not get to know the FBI agents working in the Crick personally, although I knew when they were in town and they interviewed me a couple of times.

Earlier Warren Jeffs and others were regulars on national and even a few times on world news. My prayer and support group began following the work I was doing with renewed interest. The financial support increased, and most importantly the prayer support increased.

I asked a longtime friend of mine, Pastor Dave Roberts if he knew anyone I could talk to about finding a church planter who would move to CC/H and maybe plant a church for these people who were untouched by the truth of the real Bible, not the Mormon Bible. He referred me to Pastor Chip Thompson of Ephraim, Utah. Chip suggested I contact a young man named Brody Olson who had been an intern with his ministry. Brody and his new bride Elizabeth were living in Virginia where he was finishing his last year of seminary.

In the spring of 2012, Brody Olson graduated from his seminary training in Virginia. During his senior year in seminary, I called him many times, inviting him and Elizabeth, to move to CC/H. I emphasized the need for a missionary-church planter in that community. At first, they resisted the idea, but I couldn't help myself. God was urging me to keep encouraging him to consider planting a Christ-centered church in the twin towns of CC/H.

Eventually, the Olsons heard God's call on their lives! In July 2012, Brody and Liz moved to The Crick to start their new ministry in the heart of CC/H. Oh, how evil reigned in that dark place! That didn't deter this wonderful young couple. They were sold out to the Lord.

However, they had a very serious problem finding a place to live. During that time, the FLDS Trust owned 95% of all property in and around the twin communities of CC/H. The Trust had a rule that no one was allowed to rent property to anyone, especially someone from the outside. That didn't stop the Olsons. They knew God had called them to this place, He wanted them there, and He would make a way. They trusted God to provide and He did. Miraculously, they were led to a young single mom who allowed them to move into a downstairs apartment. They could live in the apartment in exchange for remodeling the downstairs. Technically she didn't call it "rent" but said they could live there without payment while they renovated the apartment.

They faced more challenges than they expected. They were surprised when they started digging into the sheetrock and cleaning the cabinets. They found that most of the walls were covered with black mold. The Olsons ended up gutting the place, treating it, and starting over. In doing so, they made a very nice home for themselves. That little downstairs apartment was the beginning of a great ministry that God had for this community, despite its demonic stronghold.

The Olsons and I became good friends. We worked well together developing our two ministries helping and encouraging the polygamist people of CC/H. The Olsons were very welcoming to me and made sure I always had a place to stay when I went there, usually once a month.

Brody soon met a local guy named Alan. A few years earlier he was one of the first in the community to take a public stand against the FLDS. However, he paid the price. One night over a hundred men, all FLDS members, surrounded his home and physically threw him out. They took his home from him and he even ended up in jail for a short time, all based on false evidence.

A couple of years after I arrived, changes began to come to the community and Alan eventually got occupancy rights to his house. He had built the 6,000 square foot house himself. One night, Alan invited some of the locals and me to his home for a movie night. I had a great time with my new friends watching a movie and eating popcorn. Alan's living room was 1,000 square feet. The house was rough, and was far from finished.

"Who knows?" I said to Brody the next day, "Maybe someday

Alan would rent the living room to us for a Sunday worship service." At the time, the Olsons were having a Bible Study in their small downstairs apartment on Sundays. It was going very well and was the beginning of a home church.

The next surprise was when Alan was one of the first people in the community to get a legal title to his house. He realized he couldn't afford to keep the big house when his wife left him. We made arrangements with Alan to sell the house to the Olsons for an agreed upon price. The plan was that as soon as Alan got a clear title to the house, he would immediately sell it to Brody and Liz. When the day came, Alan got the legal title midmorning and he sold the house to Brody and Liz Olson by late afternoon.

Brody and Liz Olson were the first *outsiders* to become homeowners in Hildale, Utah. As far as we know, they were the *first Christian family* to become residents in the community of Short Creek.

Brody set up a legal non-profit organization called Grace Reigns and received a 501(c)3 status from the IRS. He served as chairman of Grace Reigns and asked me to serve as vice-chair of the ministry board and I accepted. The relationship between our two ministries was very cordial. In all the years we worked together we never got into a serious disagreement. I always respected him as the leader of the ministry.

Our dreams for that 1,000-square-foot living room in Alan's home came true. At first, it was the site of a Bible study and then, after a couple of years, the living room became the meeting room for Grace Community Church. A few more years passed and the large living room was too small. Then the church moved to the Grace Reigns ministry headquarters, a log building in Colorado City. The church did well in that spiritually dark community and by the end of 2019, Sunday morning attendance was averaging about 50 people; by 2023 the average attendance was nearly 100.

Brody and I worked well together. We reached out to different people groups in the CC/H area. I made friends with gray-haired folks. My goal was to encourage people to attend Brody's Bible studies and later become a part of Grace Community Church. Brody and Liz were able to reach the younger population and the youth program thrived.

In the early years of my work in the community, an attorney from Salt Lake City and I were involved in rescuing children from the FLDS, reuniting them with their mothers who had been sent away for a time of repentance. Sometimes the mothers had been separated from their children for over three years.

Another part of my work was simply to walk life with people. Even after they left the FLDS, many people found making decisions difficult. They had been told what to do, how to do it, and when to do it. There were controls over all of their activities, this extended to what to eat, what to wear, and how to use the bathroom! I listened to them, and gently made suggestions about life skills. I met with community residents in restaurants, coffee shops, and the bakery. I consumed gallons of coffee, practicing my "restaurant theology." The FLDS never banned coffee as the mainline Mormon Church did.

***

For the first eight years of my ministry with Great Commission Utah, I worked mostly with people coming out of the FLDS church. Oh, how I desired to also reach another polygamist group called the Apostolic United Brethren (AUB) better known as the "Allreds." This group was respectful and pleasant, but they did not know the Jesus of the Bible.

A few years after we started our ministry I was convinced that the second phase of the vision for Great Commission Utah was to assist people coming out of the Allreds.

We knew a family that had come out of polygamy. The children were in the public school system and the girls were not doing well.

Our son, Mitch, was the Head of School at Intermountain Christian School (ICS) in Salt Lake City. Our family all attended Christian schools growing up. Christ-centered education is a part of who we are. One day I said to Dawn, "We need to get those girls into the Christian school." I asked a few people to pay part of the tuition for the two little girls. The money came and the girls enrolled at ICS and thrived.

The next year we decided, with our board, that Great Commission Utah would raise money for tuition for more children from polygamy backgrounds. The fundraising went well; the majority of the money came from churches and individuals in Minnesota and Northwest Iowa. The new ministry within Great Commission Utah became known as the "Great Commission Utah Scholarship Fund." One year God blessed us with twelve students in the new scholarship ministry.. Seven of the students were from the Allred group.

The idea and vision for Great Commission Utah had taken root and was bearing fruit.

* * *

Sharing Jesus with people is just a part of who I am. At one point during my ministry God placed another burden on my heart, completely unassociated with the polygamy ministry. It was a personal ministry that happened when I traveled back to my home area of the Midwest, preaching in churches that supported Great Commission Utah.

I had known former Minnesota Governor Wendell R. Anderson very well. He helped me get elected to the Minnesota State House. He was a special person to me. During his time as governor, Anderson made the front page of the August 13, 1973 issue of *Time* magazine. It was predicted that one day Wendy could become a candidate for President of the United States. They listed him as the best-dressed and most popular governor in the United States.

For many years, I had a soft spot in my heart for this man. Then many years later I felt a strong urge to talk to my old friend and find out where he was in his relationship with the Lord. I contacted a former staff person of Governor Anderson, Paul Ridgeway. When I met him, he was only 21 years old and a vibrant Christian. It was great to get reacquainted with Paul. Almost forty years passed since we last spoke, but there was a special bond of Christian brotherhood between us. He helped me get in touch with the former governor.

I knew that a few weeks later, we would be in the Minneapolis area so I planned to look up my old friend. I was excited as I drove to the assisted living center, the address Paul had given me. I asked where I could find Wendell Anderson. The nurse told me he was in Room 337. I found the room; the door was open. After knocking on the door, I said in a somewhat loud voice, "Anyone home?"

"Yeah, who is it? Come on in. The door is open."

"I'm Mike Menning, former state representative and senator from Southwest Minnesota. How are you doing?"

The once Olympic gold medalist hockey player, attorney, former state representative, state senator, dignified governor, and U.S. Senator looked very different from the days I knew him. But I reminded myself, so did I some 40 years later. He was 80 years old. His curly hair was long, disheveled, and snow-white.. However, I heard the voice of the same Wendy Anderson I had known many years earlier.

We picked up where we left off. We talked for over an hour and a half and had a great conversation. I saw many books lying around and noticed a few Christian books so I asked him about the books. The former Democrat Governor said he had received the books from former Republican Governor Al Quie who was now one of his best friends. With Al Quie as his best friend, I knew Wendell Anderson was in good hands from a spiritual point of view. I shared the Gospel with Wendy and prayed with him. I promised to stay in touch and he walked me to my car.

After I left the care facility, I immediately called Paul Ridgway. Paul was ecstatic and agreed that we would stay in touch with Wendy and would continue praying for his salvation. I also called Al Quie and shared the details of my visit; he, too, was very pleased. I stayed in touch with Wendell by calling him every month. Paul and Al made regular visits to Wendell and prayed with him. Thankfully I was able to visit Wendell one more time and I felt he was close to making a commitment to the Lord. We had a great time together.

The three of us worked as a team, covering our old friend with a circle of prayer. In the early part of July, I received a call from Paul Ridgeway. He told me that while meeting with Al Quie, Wendell prayed to receive Jesus' free gift of salvation and asked Jesus to come into his heart. On July 16, about ten days after Paul called me, our old friend passed from earth to his heavenly home. Wendell R. Anderson was now safe in the arms of Jesus and I know the angels in heaven rejoiced. Luke 15:10, "Just so, I tell you, there is joy before the angels of God over one sinner who repents." [ESV]

I followed the Minnesota hot news story of the week, the passing of former Governor Anderson. Many commentators and former politicians praised the former governor. Much was said about his time in public service and some of the political mistakes he had made. Of course, there wasn't any mention of the most important news; Wendell R. Anderson accepted Jesus Christ as his personal Savior. But, there were three of us who were rejoicing and praising God that one of Jesus' lost sheep was found, and there was great rejoicing in heaven!

I praise God for touching my heart to call on my old political friend, and I was privileged to be part of a team to lead Wendell to the Lord. I am reminded of 1 Corinthians 3:5-8, "What then is Apollos? What is Paul? Servants through whom you believed, as the Lord assigned to each. I planted, Apollos watered, but God gave the growth. So neither he who plants nor he who waters is anything, but only God who gives the growth. He who plants and he who waters are one, and each will receive his wages according to his labor." [ESV]

***

On another of my ministry trips, (trip theology) in an effort to stay in touch with supporting churches, I was able to be with Mr. Martin Breems, a former teacher/mentor, as he passed from this life into the arms of Jesus. He was living in a nursing home in the little Northwest Iowa town of Sheldon. I had visited him about two years prior when he was over ninety and very bright. It was a great visit. I was seventy-three years old at the time and after fifty-four years I finally had the opportunity to tell him the truth about how my father forced me to drop out of the play that he was directing when I was a senior in high school. He said, "Teaching was difficult when working with some parents in those years."

The story doesn't end there. A year after that visit, on Sunday, October 14, 2018, I was on my way to preach at an evening service at the Sanborn Iowa Christian Reformed Church. I was driving on Iowa Highway 18 when my phone rang. Pastor Al Van Dellen, my long-time acquaintance, was calling . He asked if I had time to stop at the nursing home before the evening service to spend a few minutes with Mr. Breems who was a member of their church. The pastor explained that it looked like Mr. Breems didn't have much time left here on earth. When Mr. Breems had heard I was to be the guest speaker at the church that evening, he asked if I would be able to stop to see him. Of course, I was pleased to do so.

I pulled up to the nursing home at 5:00 p.m. The church service was to start at 6:00 p.m. When I entered his room, I immediately saw that Mr. Breems was struggling to breathe. His son Phil, his wife, and their teenage son were also there. I took Mr. Breems' hand and said, "Hi Mr. Breems, Marion Menning here."

In a very faint voice, he responded, "No, *Mike* Menning." I didn't know if he remembered me as Marion or by my nickname Mike.

He tried talking, but he didn't have the strength. I asked if I could pray with him. He nodded and tried to say, "Yes." It was a precious moment. We all held hands. I prayed to ask God to give Mr. Breems peace as he would soon pass from this world into the very presence of Jesus. His vital signs were dropping fast. Led by his son, we sang, "What a Friend We Have in Jesus." A couple of minutes later Mr. Breems stopped breathing and passed into the arms of Jesus.

I needed to leave the family and get to the church in time for the message. In those forty-five minutes from 5:00 until 5:45, God gave me a special gift. I was there at that sacred moment when someone very influential in my life passed from this world into the next.

By the time I reached the church, the service had already begun. At approximately 6:20 the pastor introduced me as the guest speaker and I explained to the congregation why I was late. I took the microphone and with a lump in my throat, I shared the wonderful moment I had holding my former teacher's hand when he passed. God had given me the topic of the evening's message about three weeks earlier, Revelations, chapter 21, which begins with, "I saw a new heaven and a new earth…"

Mr. Breems was my government teacher. It was in that class that I developed a love for the operation and role of government. Eleven years after graduation I was elected to serve in the Minnesota State House and later elected to the Minnesota State Senate. In many ways, he was more than a teacher, he was a mentor, and his influence lasted me a lifetime.

Reflections & Pondering

Section 3

Chapters 6-8

So we are Christ's ambassadors; God is making his appeal
through us. We speak for Christ when we plead,
"Come back to God."

2 Corinthians 5:20 [NLT]

Reflections on <u>Your</u> Life

Many years ago Mike prayed and pledged to God that he would go where God wanted him to go and do what He wanted him to do. Read Isaiah 6:8. Mike says, "following the Lord is not an easy task." Often when Christians are fully committed, it means the family might have to move. In Chapter 6 we read about their disabled son, Michael, who suffered from depression because of the move to Utah and his group home living conditions.

Do you think God allowed this to happen when they were following God's lead, and if so why?

When you reflect on your life have there been times when you followed God's leading and then experienced similar situations?

Do you think meeting Walmart-Bill was by chance or a divine appointment? On what do you base your answer? As you reflect on your life, are you open to asking God to bring about divine appointments in your life?

We all have times when we are tired of scam callers and could scream.

How do you feel about the way Mike handled the scam call from Nigeria? As an ambassador of Jesus, how should we handle people and circumstances that irritate us?

In reflecting on your past experiences do you think you might have missed opportunities to speak of your relationship with Jesus? Do you think God presents new mission fields, such as scam callers, to us?

The two major polygamist groups in America are the Fundamentalist Mormon groups and many in the Islam religion. As you have read a few of the stories recorded here, has God touched your heart, and asked you to consider helping to reach people in these cultures? If so, where should you begin?

Do you think it was by chance that Mike was with Mr. Breems, a very influential teacher in his life, as he passed from this world into the next? Why do you think God provided this divine appointment? What have you learned from this story?

In quick review, do you have other questions or further comments about the stories in Chapters 6, 7, or 8?

Pondering <u>Your</u> Life's Direction

How do we recognize when God is at work, calling us to get involved?

Did anything in chapters 6, 7, or 8 cause you to consider making a

Heart Change in your life, and if so, what part of the story made an impression on you?

Are there **Life Changes** you need to make to mature as an *ambassador of Jesus?* (This may be between you and God.)

Section Four

Spiritual Darkness

Nine

The Dark Swarm

For every child of God defeats this evil world, and we achieve this victory through our faith. And who can win this battle against the world? Only those who believe that Jesus is the Son of God.
1 John 5:4-5 [NLT]

Art Cooksley was just one of his father's 74 children, only one of such large FLDS families living in the Crick. When Art was in his early twenties he was able to escape the clutches of his father and the cult. Art was a very likable guy, a quiet man with honorable character, and everyone loved him. He loved having good clean fun but wasn't comfortable with all the rules of the FLDS. One day, Art simply packed the few things he owned, left town, and put the FLDS in his rearview mirror. Art didn't make a phone call to his father until late in the afternoon when he was several hundred miles down the road. He knew it was safe for him because he didn't say where he was or where he was headed. He knew the god squad couldn't find him at that point. After a long day's drive, he arrived in the Phoenix area. By nightfall, he got to his brother's house. His father would no longer have control over him. It was tough for his father to keep track of all his children!

Art soon found a good job. It felt great for him to realize he no longer had to give the entire paycheck to the FLDS church. He saved his money and life was going well. Art met Mary, a beautiful young lady, and they were soon married. God blessed them with two wonderful children.

Late one afternoon, Mary got a call from the police telling her that while on his road construction job, Art had been hit by a car and was admitted to the ICU at the Scottsdale Medical Center. Mary left their children with her mother and headed to the hospital. She was shocked when she entered his room. She couldn't even recognize her husband. He was in very bad condition, on life support, and not expected to make it through the night.

After a week, the doctor said he thought Art would live, but would likely never walk again. Indeed, the accident left Art permanently disabled. Praise God, three months later Art walked out of the hospital with the assistance of a walker. His speech was slurred and he had a hard time getting his thoughts out in a way that people could understand. But praise God, his cognitive functions were intact.

His brothers never forgot him and encouraged Art and Mary to move back to The Crick because they were willing to help and look after their brother.

Several years before, Warren Jeffs ordered that all construction on private houses had to stop. All effort was to be put into building Jeffs' residence for he and his many, many wives. At that time there were over ninety houses that were at various stages of completion. The church owned these houses and almost all the property in Colorado City and Hildale. The property was controlled in a trust, the United Effort Plan (UEP).

When the Cooksleys returned to the Crick, Art and Mary petitioned the Trust to be granted permission to purchase one of those unfinished houses on the edge of town. The house was only 40% completed, framed with windows and a roof. To the surprise of many, the Trust sold the house to the Cooksley family. A couple of Art's brothers, the contractors, got together and in a short time, finished the house. It was ready for Art and his family to move in. Art and Mary were more excited about life than they had been since the time of the accident. They had the official deed and they had a new home.

However, there were two major problems. The water and sewer were not hooked up. Art and Mary went to the city council seeking a permit for water and sewer to be brought from the street to the house. The city council, which was controlled by the FLDS, told them that everything was in order and assured them that they would soon have water and sewer. The Cooksleys wrote a check for the fees and went home.

Days passed but they heard nothing from the city. They went back to the city offices and realized they were getting a runaround. It was all beginning to feel like a nightmare. Days turned into weeks, and weeks into months followed by another month. Still no water or sewer. They purchased an old truck, mounted a used water tank on it, parked it in front of the house, and connected it to the house with a hose. As for the sewer, the city wouldn't allow them to hook into the city sewer system. Like in the old days, they used a chamber pot in the "bathroom" and had to carry it out back to dump it.

They knew that since the City Council was controlled by the FLDS Church and since the Cooksleys were not members in good standing with the FLDS, the city was not about to move quickly in hooking up the water and sewer.

The city not only wouldn't hook them up, but they harassed the Cooksleys. One morning, at about seven o'clock, they heard a commotion outside. They looked out the windows and the city employees were unloading a track hoe and a backhoe. The Cooksleys were excited, assuming finally the city was going to hook up water and sewer. But it was not so! The city workers dug trenches all around their property. Mary called the police, but the FLDS controlled them as well. The police arrived on the scene and warned the Cooksleys not to get involved. The police were there to protect the city employees, not the Cooksleys. That was only the beginning of the harassment.

The Cooksleys decided to take the city council to court. As usual, the city hired the finest and most expensive attorneys. The city had been involved in this sort of lawsuit before and was ready for a fight, all at the taxpayer's expense.

By then, the Cookleys and I had become friends. For months, we prayed for justice to prevail in the upcoming court trial. We prayed for the family, the city council, and Art's health.

The trial lasted more than a week. I prayed and many others in our ministry joined in prayer. During the trial, neither the Cooksleys nor their attorney ever asked for an amount of money to be awarded. Finally, after a long deliberation, the jury came with a verdict. They found the city guilty on all charges! The jury ordered the city to provide water and sewer for the Cooksleys and, to the surprise of everyone, the jury awarded them several million dollars. In the end, they received about half the amount.

The trial was over, they were soon hooked up to water and sewer! Life for the Cooksleys was getting back to normal. It seemed as though they were more relaxed when I visited them. I had more opportunities to gain the trust of the family. We found ourselves discussing spiritual matters. I was hoping they would come to Sunday worship and Bible study at Brody and Liz's place.

During this time, my "home away from home" was the back office in the log building which was used as a community center and operated by Grace Reigns. It served a two-fold purpose, as an office, and I had brought a good used hide-a-bed couch for sleeping.

One evening, I received a call from Mary asking if I had time to come over to the house to talk with them. I was pretty excited. I jumped in my red truck and headed over. We talked for a while at the island in the dining area. Mary asked if I believed in demons and if I had ever dealt with them. I told them a little history of how God had placed me in situations where I had to cast demons out of homes. On several occasions, God had used me to release people from demonic strongholds, even though I didn't like dealing with this. I praise God for a few very dear pastor friends who had taught me that only people who had given their lives to Jesus were given the authority to cast out demons and that it only can be done through the name of Jesus Christ.

Mary shared the story of what she assumed was a demonic presence in their home. Art and Mary led me to a bedroom just down the hall. I sensed they were somewhat uneasy showing me a particular closet. They were not using that closet because of some bad experiences their family had since they had moved into the house. I could tell they were pretty frightened. Art's brothers told them that when they were finishing the interior construction of the house they could hardly finish that closet. The sheet rockers and painters also expressed that there was just something very weird and scary about working in that closet.

The room was supposed to be their daughter's bedroom. On the very first night when they moved in, their daughter got up after a few hours and slept on the couch for the remainder of the night. She had not been able to sleep in the bedroom since then. Others tried sleeping there as well, but it simply wasn't restful.

When we opened the closet door I could feel something. I knew what was going on immediately. My skin began getting a prickly feeling from the top of my head down my back and legs. I knew this situation all too well. Something like this happened to me every time I was in the presence of a demon's stronghold. I knew what we were facing and I didn't like it. But God put on my heart that I had to deal with it properly, in the power of the Lord Jesus. I was not to turn away!

I knew what had to be done. I asked Art and Mary to stand with me while I prayed to clear the place of the demons in their home. I prayed, reminding God, as if He needed reminding, that it was clear in the Scripture that demons cannot stand against the power and presence of Jesus. As we prayed, I felt I was growing closer and closer to Jesus.

I prayed in the name of Jesus, commanding the evil to leave. I made that command, not with any power of my own, but through the power of Jesus and the Holy Spirit. In Jesus' name, I commanded the spirits to leave immediately and never return. We waited and yes, we could feel it, they were gone! (Later I realized I should have prayed and commanded through the authority of God that the demons would present themselves to Jesus upon leaving, I didn't and I realized later that night, that it would cost me.) We thanked God. Then with oil, I anointed the closet, the bedroom, and the house asking God to seal that place, making it impossible for the demons to return.

We sat in the dining area and prayed again thanking God for what He had done. We could feel a sense of peace in that house. I left the house and got in my truck. The sense of peace did not last long. As I left to go back to the log building I felt the presence of evil. It was as though the demons were following me. It felt like something was crawling over my skin. I once again had goosebumps from head to toe.

I entered the log building and walked to the back room. I was overwhelmed. I could feel demons everywhere and my spirit was agitated. I could feel goosebumps all over my body, even worse than earlier. I fell to my knees next to the bed and cried out to God, *In the name and the power of Jesus, I command you to leave.* Nothing happened. I was being tormented and, even though I prayed fervently, nothing seemed to help. I was terrified and didn't know what to do. I didn't know why God didn't just kick them out of that place!

I grabbed my toiletries and my clothing, and threw them in my suitcase. I walked to the front entrance, locked the door, jumped in my pick-up, and headed out of town. After going three or four miles I suddenly felt at peace. They were gone. That night I drove to Hurricane and checked into a hotel.

It was about eleven o'clock when I called Dawn. I didn't know where to start. She was aware of my experience with demonic attacks and how I had previously helped people to get rid of them. I told her that this evening was different. I explained how I had prayed in the log building, my home away from home, and nothing seemed to make a difference. She agreed to pray for me and assured me that all would be okay.

Sleep didn't come easily that night, for me or Dawn! It seemed like I was dealing with bad nightmares much of the night. I got up around six the next morning, showered, grabbed some breakfast, and headed back up the mountain toward the Crick.

I went back to my office/bedroom and everything appeared normal. Midmorning my phone rang. It was Mary Cooksley.

"Mike, we were wondering if you could stop over. We would like to talk a little about last night."

"Sure," I said, "I'll be there in about 15 minutes." I was about to find out what happened the night before as I left their home. They invited me in and we sat around the curved island in the dining area again. She and Art explained that after I left, they went back to the bedroom closet and they could feel it was calm and peaceful.

"But Mike, how are you doing?"

I started explaining but didn't get very far when Mary interrupted. "We saw what happened last night when you left."

I was confused. "What do you mean?"

Mary explained that she and Art were looking out the window watching me leave the house as the sun was about to set. They said that as I went down the street it looked like an angry dark cloud swirled around my truck and continued down the street. I was amazed and knew what the angry-looking cloud was. God opened the eyes of the Cooksleys to see the dark swarm. They said, maybe the best way to describe it was to compare it to awakening a hornet's nest. Only this time, through the power of God, I had stirred up a demon's nest that had been comfortable where it had been hiding for a while.

The explanation of the dark cloud following me is exactly what attacked me the night before. Art and Mary were deeply appreciative that I came to rid them of the stronghold, yet at the same time apologized for putting me through the terror of the night before.

I had a new question to deal with. Why had I been so terrorized that night before? Why was I not able to cast them out once I reached my place? Later that day, I left for home trying to make sense of all this.

To add insult to injury, the next Sunday morning our pastor, Dave, preached on the subject of how to respond when evil attacks us. "Never run from demons," he said.

Wow, Dave, now there is a kick to the gut when I am already down, I argued in my head. *But, Dave, I did run. It seemed like there was a legion of demons and it was terrifying. So, what should I have done?*

The worship service finished with the worship team singing, "Great I Am," a beautiful song by Phillips, Craig, and Dean. As I was worshiping and singing, some lyrics of the song hit me with another blow:

The mountains shake before you
The demons run in fear
At the mention of the name King of Majesty

I cried out to God from my innermost being. *Please, Lord, show me. Was my running from evil a couple of nights ago a victory for Satan?* Praise God, the demons never went back to the Cooksleys. But what about all that happened to me that night?

I was led to Mark 9:28-29. "After Jesus had gone indoors, his disciples asked him privately, 'Why couldn't we drive it out?' He replied, 'This kind can come out only by prayer.'" [NIV] I searched further and discovered that the older translations, the KJV and the NKJV, say, "only through prayer and fasting." In another situation recorded in Matthew, Jesus told the disciples it was because they didn't have enough faith. Because of my fear, I wondered, had I faltered in my faith?

I pondered the question for a long time. At the house it was through the blood and power of Jesus and the Holy Spirit that the demons left, but why not in my office/bedroom a half-hour later? I finally concluded that I panicked in that office.

A powerful lesson was hammered into me that day. I should have used what the Bible teaches, but I didn't. I should have stood my ground and faced the demons head-on. Luke 10:17 says, "The seventy-two returned with joy, saying, 'Lord, even the demons are subject to us in your name!'" [ESV] I should have prayed and asked God for miraculous power and cast the demons out of that place and sent them to Jesus!

In those two days, this missionary learned something new. I was reminded that the war between us and Satan has already been won by Christ through His death on the cross and His resurrection. But we must continue to fight the battles here on earth. Through the power and name of Jesus Christ and the Holy Spirit, God has given us the authority to kick out demons, we must fight our fears of evil for it is through the blood of Jesus and His resurrection that the power of Satan has been defeated.

Make no mistake about it, we are never to treat lightly the God-given authority that Christ has given to His children. The scripture says, "But even Michael, one of the mightiest of the angels, did not dare accuse the devil of blasphemy, but simply said, 'The Lord rebuke you.'" Jude 1:9 [NLT]

Oh, yes there are times, even in our dedication to serving Jesus, that Satan doesn't give up on tempting and harassing us. As old as I am, Satan continues his attack on me. It usually comes to me at night in demonic and terrifying nightmares. God is so good and gives us victory over evil. Yes, Pastor Dave was right in saying; we should never run from demons.

Ten

The Big Dark House

*When an evil spirit leaves a person, it goes into the desert,
seeking rest but finding none. Then it says, "I will return to the
person I came from." So it returns and finds its former home empty,
swept, and in order. Then the spirit finds seven other spirits more
evil than itself, and they all enter the person and live there...*
Matthew 12: 43-45 [NLT]

The world of demonic, fallen angels as the Bible describes it, is
a very real thing in today's world; just as it has been since the
fall of man in the Garden of Eden. I experienced a head-on meeting
with demons on numerous occasions in my life. The worst and heaviest
oppression during such unusual encounters gave me feelings of the
presence of demonic creatures. I went on an assessment visit with
CRWRC to Somalia in the late 90s, a couple of months after the U.S.
Marines landed on their shores. We were there under the umbrella of
Samaritan's Purse for ten days. Our ministry was assisting with food
distribution and providing basic health care.

The demonic presence was so evident there that it was outright
creepy; it felt like the demons were crawling everywhere. The evil was
wreaking havoc and causing severe food shortages as thousands of
people died of starvation every day. When the United States Marines
first arrived, one of their first jobs was to pick up the bodies of men,

women, and children that lay on the roadsides in Mogadishu. There were hundreds upon hundreds of wild dogs ripping the bodies apart before the Marines could get to them. The Marines dug trenches and brought the bodies to the trenches. I saw dogs digging up shallow graves in that city. It was there that I first witnessed an almost green glow of the devil's presence in the eyes of a few adults and even some children.

Somalia was the darkest place I ever experienced, and the next was the "dark house" in Colorado City/Hildale.

When I refer to the "dark house" I am referring to the house of Warren Jeffs, the Fundamentalist Latter Day Saints Church's prophet. I consider him a demonic leader. He was the iron-fisted "dictator" of the FLDS, living in CC/H until he went underground for nearly three years while on the FBI's Most Wanted List. During that time the FLDS legally owned about 95% of all the property in and around CC/H. Upon Jeff's arrest, the property was taken over by the United Effort Plan Trust (UEP), a non-profit, 501-C-3. After his arrest, much of Jeff's organization began coming apart at the seams.

After many federal court hearings, the court turned the operation of the Trust over to the Attorney Generals of Utah and Arizona. After much discussion, it was agreed that the office of the Utah Attorney General would take over and appoint a citizens board to administer its operation. As a result of these actions, the newly appointed board of the UEP passed a rule that former owners of the properties would have first right of refusal to gain legal ownership of the properties. One of the properties was a very, very, large home. It had over 50 bedrooms, a food storage kitchen, a large commercial kitchen, and over 50 bathrooms. It had been the home of the FLDS prophet Warren Jeffs and many of his wives and children.

We got to know a few of the former wives of Jeffs who escaped after his arrest. Attorney Ron Poole, a few others, and I met with one of the former wives. She had no assets or property to her name. Together we helped her write up a proposal to the UEP Board asking that the property be given to her to be used to help former "sister wives" in their recovery, after many of them had been drugged and seriously abused. The board voted to legally give her the enormous house. Later I assisted her in transferring the property to another ministry which turned it into a ministry center for many women and their families who had left the polygamy culture, including other former wives of the Jeffs' cult.

Throughout this process, I gained access to the property and the house. When I entered that huge house with the new owner and several others, I experienced something I had not bargained for! As we went through the house I could feel the demonic presence of evil.

On my first tour of the house, a former FLDS person served as our guide. He had helped build the property so he knew every nook and cranny in the place. He showed us several of the bedroom doors which had heavy-duty reverse locks. The doors could only be unlocked in the hallway, from the outside of the room. I already knew why those locks were in place. I had seen something similar in other polygamist houses. Disobedient wives were routinely locked in their bedrooms for various lengths of time depending on how Jeffs sentenced them. One of Jeffs's former wives shared that she had been locked in her room for three months and was not able to see her children for that entire time.

The house had three levels; garden view, main floor, and upper level. I was taken to the garden view level and shown a nice room, it had bookshelves on the wall opposite the door. Our "tour guide" asked us to examine the bookshelves. I searched the shelves very carefully and saw nothing unusual. Then he braced himself against one end of the middle section of shelves and asked me to pull the other end. I squeezed my fingers between the two upright units and was able to pull that end of the shelf forward. It swung apart from the other two sets of shelves. The well-designed shelf rested on very precise, expensive rollers opening into an inner room. I looked into the new opening and saw a closed door. Our tour guide said, "Go ahead, open the door." I did, and there was a room with concrete floors, walls, and ceiling. It had vents bringing in fresh air from the outside. There were only a few furnishings. Another doorway led to a tunnel that we learned was connected to a house on the northwest corner of that square block, and was the home of Rulon Jeffs, Warren's father. Months later I was shown the father's gigantic house and saw where the secret passage connected to Warren's house.

For the next several months when I visited the Crick, I spent time going through every part of the dark house, and I prayed for cleansing from evil. Sometimes I was alone and sometimes with one or two others. We prayed from room to room.

The darkest and most evil of all the rooms was Warren's bedroom. It was a little nicer and had a much thicker carpet. When I entered that room I felt goosebumps from the top of my head to my toes. I knew I was battling demons. I prayed earnestly in the name and power of the risen Jesus, commanding evil to leave and sending them to appear before Jesus. On one occasion Dawn was with me; she became physically ill when she entered that room and was unable to stay.

Another spiritually dark room was the first room to the right of the entrance on the main floor. We entered the room with one of the young, former wives who told us about how it was in that room that she was humiliated on her wedding day. She explained that her wedding was held in the late afternoon, with only a few of the FLDS leaders, her parents, and some of Warren's other wives present. Her sisters were not invited. By that time Warren had "only" about 50 or 60 wives. After the wedding meal Warren and she made a couple of phone calls to her sisters. There was no greater honor given to any family than having one of a family's daughters marry Jeffs because they were taught that Jeffs was *God*. So in their minds, the family was then considered to be a part of the Godhead. Some believed that Jeffs was even considered the third person in the Trinity, and even higher than the Holy Spirit.

After the phone calls and things were settling down, Warren took her to the special room. He took his place of honor in a large chair in one corner. He told her to stand in front of him and take off her clothes. She told us she was very nervous and shaking from head to toe. Girls in the culture were never taught anything about sex, because that was the duty of the new husband to whom they would be assigned. She hesitated, and the prophet became disturbed and yelled at her to remove all her clothing and stand naked before him. He told her that he needed to look her over. Shaking, she complied, because as the wife of the prophet, it was her duty to "keep sweet." Those words even stand out on the chimney of the house, all shaped with dark bricks against the lighter bricks of the chimney. He instructed her to turn around a couple of times, and then he yelled for a couple of wives who were waiting just outside the door. They came in and he said, "Get her out of here, bring, (he named one of the other wives) into my bedroom." His new wife was banned from his sex harem and served as a slave wife. She explained that only about half of the wives were sex wives. The others were assigned to be worker wives.

This young lady endured unbelievable abuse. She had to work from four in the morning until well into the night, every day for several years. One night she tried to escape by scaling the 12-foot wall that surrounded the property, dropping on the other side, and running to the safety of her family, only to be returned to the demonic cult.

After learning first-hand about the power of this monstrous demonic cult leader, I realized there were no limits to his evil. I also learned never to underestimate the power of anyone who has given their life to satanic forces.

At that time I knew I was facing a powerful evil force in that big empty house. A couple of committed Christians joined me to pray to cast out the demons, not in our authority, but we had to claim the authority Jesus has over demons. I was reminded of Matthew 12:43-45 which tells us, "When an evil spirit leaves a person, it goes into the desert, seeking rest but finding none. Then it says, 'I will return to the person I came from.' So it returns and finds its former home empty, swept, and in order. Then the spirit finds seven other spirits more evil than itself, and they all enter the person and live there…" [NLT] This passage refers to the expelling of evil from a person, but I believe the same principle applies to throwing evil out of places once inhabited by the devil and his hosts.

After many prayer walks, I began to feel victory of Jesus in that house. A group of us anointed the place with oil in the name of the Father, the Son, and the Holy Spirit, sealing it in Jesus' name.

This enormous house could drain the finances from almost anyone's budget and the new owner, the former wife of Jeffs, had no money for upkeep, taxes, and utilities. Then a miracle happened. The Dream Church, the founder of Dream Centers around the world, offered to help. This wonderful group of Christians moved ahead. A couple of us worked with the young lady and this group to gain legal ownership of the property for a new Dream Center. They would open a shelter for women and children who came out of the demonic FLDS. The Dream Center also provided employment and shelter for former wives and children of Warren Jeffs.

Since the acquisition of that property, the Christian ministry of The Dream Center has helped to bring the light of Jesus to the dark community of Colorado City, Arizona, and Hildale, Utah. I continue to be amazed when thinking about that enormous house, one of the darkest places I have ever experienced, was a former home of legends of fallen angels, and a place of torture and a slavery stronghold of women. Now, it is a center of ministry in the name of our Lord Jesus Christ. Truly, Jesus is the victor over the devil and all his hosts.

The Lord has blessed the ministry of Brody and Liz Olson as they also bring the light of Jesus to this dark community through the ministries of Grace Reigns and the Grace Community Church. Together both ministries are making a difference in Colorado City/ Hildale. The Grace Community Church is today a healthy church with an average Sunday morning attendance of around 100. The Grace Reigns Community Center provides after-school programs for the youth and a community thrift store which is often the first point of contact with people from the community.

Yes, these Christian ministries are truly a beacon of light in what once was a very dark community.

Eleven

"They're Coming for My Children"

...All the days ordained for me were written in your book
before one of them came to be.
Psalm 139:16 [NIV]

On a hot summer day when I was in CC/H, we were about to start a board meeting of Grace Reigns. I happened to look out the window and saw a lady running toward our building. Five children were running as fast as they could, trying to keep up with their mom who was racing at a frantic pace. "They're coming to take my children, they're going to get the rest of my children!" She was yelling at the top of her voice!

Miriam was a single mother, a former plural wife. The FLDS had sent her polygamist husband away "to repent from afar." Like so many before her, Mariam would also be sent away. The FLDS had already claimed her two oldest children, girls ages 13 and 15; the favorite ages of the FLDS leadership's potential wives.

That day three men of the FLDS came to her home where she and her children were living, which happened to be only a block from the log building where we were. The men said they came on behalf of the "church," sent by the prophet. They said that all seven of her children were the responsibility of the church, and since the children were owned by the church, the church would be claiming them. They said she had signed her children over to the FLDS Church at the time her husband had been sent away to repent from afar. We knew the church required the moms to sign many documents. Many women were not able to read well enough to understand what they were being asked to sign. Keeping people illiterate was part of the church's strategy to maintain power.

She wisely asked the men for a copy of the documents that she supposedly had signed. They left to get the documents and said they would be back in an hour. They also implied that if she cared at all about the salvation of her children and herself, she would not oppose them taking the children. When the men left she grabbed her five children and ran for the ministry center. At this moment, it was a house of refuge to her.

We knew we had to act quickly. I called the Mohave County Sheriff's office and told them what was happening. The situation in Colorado City was so volatile that the Sheriff's Office had assigned 24/7 protection, basically for the sake of those leaving the FLDS. There were two deputies in town that day. Within five minutes they showed up at our office and Miriam explained the situation. We asked them to stay at the ministry center and give protection to the five children while we left to rescue the two older daughters.

Brody Olson proceeded with the board meeting knowing the situation was under control.

The two older daughters were in the care of a FLDS caretaker who had been placed in charge of a house full of girls. I estimate the ages of the girls in that house were from 12 to 15. This particular caretaker's house was north, just a few blocks up the street from the ministry center; legally, in the town of Hildale, Utah. For all practical purposes, Colorado City/Hildale look like one town, but the state lines of Utah and Arizona run through the town on a street named Uzona

Avenue.

I made two phone calls. The first was to Ron Poole, the attorney in Salt Lake City. He advised me to have sheriff's protection from Washington County on the Utah side. The second call was to Holding Out Help to ask them to immediately find a "safe house" for Miriam and her seven children. The attorney recommended that we take the mom to the caretaker's house, with the deputy's protection, and tell the caretaker in no uncertain terms that if he didn't produce the girls to their mother we would immediately file kidnapping charges against him.

Miriam and I went to the house. The Washington County Deputy was already there and the girls were outside. The house had a five-foot wall around it. Miriam and I went to the fence. Miriam called for her daughters to come immediately. The youngest daughter made a beeline for her mother and climbed over the fence to the safety of her mother's arms. The oldest daughter and the other girls living at that location ran into the house.

The caretaker of this house was a big man called "Big Mike" who came out of the house. There was no doubt – he was in control! And, he was very upset. He confronted me – nose to nose. With all the authority I could gather and the deepest voice I could muster up, I repeated the words Attorney Ron Poole told me to say, "We are in contact with a Washington County judge and as we speak Attorney Poole is drawing up the papers to ask for a warrant to be issued for your arrest on the charges of kidnapping. If you cooperate with us immediately we will stop the process. But if you don't, you could be behind bars for many years." He looked at the deputy standing a few yards to my right.

Big Mike backed down, he looked at me, knowing I meant business, and at an accelerated pace went straight for the house. About thirty seconds later he came out with the oldest daughter. He opened the gate, and the girl walked through the gate to the safety of her mother who was waiting. I breathed a sigh of relief knowing these two girls would not be given to one of the at least 60-year-old cronies of the prophet, as a 5th, or who knows, the 10th plural wife. We put the girls in the back seat of my pickup truck and headed to the ministry center.

Back at the ministry center Brody's sister, Ruth, had already made arrangements to get the mom and her seven children out of town. Within minutes, they were leaving town with a deputy sheriff's escort. About twenty minutes later they turned north on I-15 toward Salt Lake City.

The family was back together and under the care of Ruth Olson. Ruth, in her mid-twenties, was a rock-solid Christian. She was a tall, very attractive, well-educated Wyoming cowgirl who wore blue jeans, a western shirt, and cowboy boots. What people didn't know about Ruth was that inside one of those boots she carried her pistol. No male chauvinist FLDS man would want to mess with this young lady! She could take care of herself. Ruth was working for Holding Out Help at the time. Another person from Holding Out Help planned to meet them halfway on I-15. They would take Miriam and the children to a safe house in Draper, Utah.

We continued our board meeting that afternoon and by evening I received word that Miriam and the girls were safely in their new home about 280 miles north. A whole new life lay ahead of them.

Those early days of ministry were sometimes action-filled. That evening as I settled in for the night I thanked the Lord that I was able to be used as a tool in the hands of my Maker once again. I believe I have the spiritual gift of standing firm for issues of justice, as Jesus stood for justice. God was truly molding me to become more mature as an ambassador of Jesus. I praised God that when it is hard to know what to do while under pressure it's good to know and recognize the Good Shepherd's voice as He leads me. John 10:27 says, "My sheep hear my voice, and I know them, and they follow me." [ESV]

***

At that time Attorney Ron Poole and I got together for breakfast monthly to catch up on what was happening down in The Crick. We met at the Intermountain Medical Center Hospital Cafeteria. We knew it was a safe place to talk and no one would be trying to eavesdrop.

At one of those meetings, Ron shared with me that he and an investigator from the Washington County Sheriff's office were planning a big child rescue in Hildale. A judge there granted legal documents that allowed them to enter a house where they thought children were being held by the FLDS. Ron asked me if I would be willing to help in the operation. He shared as much of the plan with me as he could, although many of the details were being kept under wraps because they suspected that the FLDS had a mole in the deputies of the sheriff's department.

Ron called me a couple of days later and said the details were in place. The plan was for five mothers; eight deputies; the head detective; two attorneys; Sam Brower, the private detective; and I to meet at the Washington County Sheriff's complex about halfway between Hurricane and St. George, Utah. (Strange but true, the city is officially named Purgatory.) He said once we were assembled, the plan would be reviewed and, if everything worked as planned, we would rescue 19 children from the hands of the FLDS and reunite them with their mothers. Once we entered Hildale, the operation would be carried out with utmost speed.

I was asked to come with a twelve-passenger van which I borrowed from our son Mitch. The plan was that I should take one mom, her sister, and the mom's four children back to Spanish Fork to the home of Pastor Matthew Anderson and his wife, Chandra. The Andersons were church planters and served on our Board of Directors of Great Commission Utah.

When I arrived at the sheriff's office, I was told to hide the van behind a large berm near the back of the complex. I would leave my van at the sheriff's office and ride in one of the squad cars on the way to CC/H. There were ten county police officers and each knew exactly which house they were assigned to.

At exactly eight o'clock that morning, we arrived at CC/H where we met the mother of the four boys, Luci Neilson, and her two sisters. All three and an undercover female deputy were dressed in prairie dresses and had their hair done up FLDS style. It was a disguise so they would blend into the FLDS community. Eight marked squad cars, the detective's car, Sam's car, and Ron, who was driving his truck were all part of the plan. Attorney John Madison, a Christian friend of mine, and I took our places. John was stationed at the front entrance and I was at the back entrance of the house as two deputies entered the front door. As they entered, I saw someone taking the kids out of the backdoor. I phoned for help. A deputy went after them and had them all back in a matter of about ten minutes.

Just as the mom was being reunited with her children, Ron pulled up in his truck and called for me to come with him. I jumped in. "This is not according to plan," I said, confused.

"Oh, yes, it is," Ron smiled. "This is the real plan. The other was a decoy plan because there was a mole among the deputies and we couldn't trust them. He had close ties with the FLDS."

We went to the house where Luci and her four little boys were coming out of the house. The officers rushed her and the boys into a squad car. I jumped into a squad car behind them. We sped out of town and headed back to the sheriff's complex about twenty-five miles to the west. The deputies were talking back and forth about how we stirred up a hornet's nest of the FLDS god squad. Both of the squad cars arrived at the Sheriff's complex at the same time. They pulled behind the complex next to my van. One of Luci's sisters left to return home.

Luci, her sister from Salt Lake City, and the four boys were transferred into my van. The deputy gave me final instructions before we headed out. He said he would escort me up to Interstate 15 because the FLDS god squad was circling the area looking for the person who had taken the children. Once we got to I-15 he said I should pull off at every exit that had an overpass for the first thirty miles. If they were following us, they would either follow us up the off-ramp or they would be forced to go on to the next exit. By that time I would have the opportunity to lose them. I had to stay in phone contact with the sheriff's deputy until I came to Cedar City which is about 35 miles north. I did as instructed and everything worked out fine, we successfully lost the god squad.

Luci had been sent away to repent by the FLDS three years before this time. The youngest was only a year old when Luci was forced out. The two youngest children didn't even remember their mother. She was so happy and overwhelmed, all at the same time. Luci's sister was a great help and everything was going well.

Since none of us had eaten since breakfast and the children were hungry by the time we got to Cedar City, we decided to stop at Panda Express for carry-out and eat as we drove on, adding miles between CC/H and us. We went inside and stood in line. Great Commission Utah picked up the tab. I sensed that something didn't feel quite right. We got back in the van and headed up I-15. "There was something strange about the way people at Panda Express were looking at me," I said.

"What do you mean?" Luci asked.

"Well, some of the people gave me nasty looks and it just seemed as if everyone's eyes were glued to us, especially me."

"Duh, Mike, here you were, a gray-haired man in his late sixties with two young ladies with FLDS hairdos and wearing prairie dresses with four little boys." Luci was laughing. "Why do you think they were giving you those dirty looks?"

I laughed too and couldn't believe it. How could I be so naive?

I guess I had become accustomed and comfortable with the people I was ministering to. I was consumed by the day's rescue effort that I hadn't thought of how I must have looked in the eyes of the public. I am sure they assumed that I was just one of those dirty old men from The Crick who had taken two young brides and lived a polygamist lifestyle.

We were hungry and eager to get down the road. We had a long way to go before the end of the day.

The next laugh was about a hundred miles down the road. After an hour and a half, the kids had to use the restroom so I pulled over at a convenience store. We took turns watching if any of the FLDS were catching up with us.

As I was leaving the convenience store, I met a young lady at the door. "Mike, I think we're ready to go," she said. I was a little startled. *Who was this lady?*

Luci had her second laugh. She and her sister had changed out of their prairie dresses, into their "normal" clothes, and let their hair down. I didn't even recognize them.

An hour or two further down the road the little boys fell asleep. Luci was in the seat just behind me. She talked most of the way to Anderson's home. She told me about her polygamist husband and all the belittlement, criticism, and rule keeping she had to endure. Luci and her boys were quickly becoming friends of ours, a friendship that would last a lifetime.

Her husband was just one of the hundreds of men who were taken to other locations, leaving their families behind to fend for themselves. These men had to work hard to make all the money they possibly could and send it to the FLDS church. They were required to work 12-14 hours a day. The men nearly starved as they sent no money home to their families and almost all to the FLDS headquarters. This was part of "repenting from afar" which was the only way of getting back into the FLDS and, as they were taught, their only chance of regaining their salvation.

Luci was blessed because when she had to leave, her four little boys were given to her mom, the children's grandmother. Her mother's last words to her were, "I will take good care of the boys and will not turn them against you, regardless of what the church says." Her mother stuck to her word. Her two oldest sons were glad to see their mom. Although the two youngest did not remember her, they watched their older brothers' joy as they became reacquainted with their mom.

A little after ten that night, we arrived at the home of the Andersons in Spanish Fork. We moved the family into the house. Luci and her sister took the children downstairs and tucked them in. The Andersons were our good friends. I brought them up to date on the happenings of the day. Finally, I went down to say goodbye to the boys and then to Luci and her sister. I left and headed for home.

I didn't get tired as I drove the last fifty miles of the day's big journey. I rejoiced and praised God for the wonderful work he had called me to and how I was able to serve Him. It was such an incredible blessing to be able to know that I was in the center of where God wanted me in my service to the Master.

My thoughts went back to one of my favorite Bible passages, Psalm 139:16, "....All the days ordained for me were written in your book before one of them came to be." [NIV] At a little past midnight, I drove the borrowed van up to our home. I had put in over eighteen hours; it was a good, but, long day. I kept Dawn updated on what was happening throughout the day. I was anxious to fill her in on all the details, but when I arrived at our home, she was already sleeping. The next morning at breakfast I shared the joys and some anxious moments of the previous day.

Two days later Attorney Ron Poole and I met for breakfast. He informed me that we didn't get all 19 kids reunited with their mothers. Fifteen children were reunited with their mothers that day. One of the moms of four children backed out because of fear of the false teachings of the FLDS; she believed that if she carried through with the plan she and her children would spend eternity lost and in hell. This made me sad and angry about Satan's work.

Holding Out Help did a great job getting Luci settled in another state where she went to school and was able to get a good job. God opened many doors for her and her four boys. She was safe at last, and is now living in Texas. Luci is committed to the Lord, giving Him all the credit for saving her and her children. We have stayed in touch with Luci and consider her a great friend.

Even though the father of the children got off with no consequences, he finally stopped harassing her. We continue to pray for Luci and her boys who are growing into fine young men. They, too, have a new life, forever away from the FLDS.

Twelve

The Clay Family - Was It Worth It?

*Other seeds fell on rocky ground, where they did not have much
soil, and immediately they sprang up, since they had no depth
of soil, but when the sun rose they were scorched. And since they
had no root, they withered away.*
Matthew 13:5-6 [ESV]

After a very busy week, I sat down to relax on a Saturday evening around 8:00. As the old saying goes, "I was tired to the bone." My phone rang.

"Hello, Mike. Spencer Clay here."

"It's good to hear your voice."

"I know I have not treated you well in the past, just pulling out and not telling you about us moving my family up here to Idaho. You were on vacation, and I didn't tell you where we were …" his voice trailed off. "I also want you to know that I am sorry for standing you up when you made that trip up here a month ago to see my family and me. But Mike, I need help and was wondering if you could help."

I could not help but recollect that we had spent more time, money, and involvement with this family than any others during our ministry. Our relationship and friendship had ended abruptly when Spencer dropped us like a hot potato.

"Well, Spencer, what's on your mind?"

"I am wondering if you would help me get my three minor daughters out of the FLDS." They were daughters of his first wife who was still in the FLDS. They were living with their oldest brother, Spencer's son, and his family in Colorado City.

Despite how tired I was and how he had treated me in the past, I was after all an ambassador of Jesus and I knew what Jesus would do. I told him I would help and asked about his timeline. He said he was already on his way from Idaho headed to Colorado City and asked if I could meet him there no later than 10:30 the next morning. I thought to myself, *tomorrow is Sunday, I want to go to worship and be with my family. But, Spencer has a great need,* so I agreed to help him get his daughters back.

I hung up the phone and groaned. It meant that I had to be on the road by 5:30 the next morning, Sunday. I usually kept Sundays open since it was my day with Michael and Dawn, but that is the way things go sometimes when you are in the ministry. Oh, the life of a missionary!

The next morning I left home at 5:30. I arrived at our agreed-upon meeting place right at the agreed time, 320 miles from our home. I asked Spencer if he knew exactly where the girls were. He said he did.

Next, I asked what the plan was. "Mike, that's why I needed you here. I have no plan."

Even though each of the rescues was different, the basics were always the same. I laid out a plan. First, we contacted the Mohave County Sheriff's Office, explained the situation to them, and asked them to be present to provide cover for us.

Within an hour we moved into position. Spencer and I went to the door and walked into the house of his oldest son, a faithful follower of the FLDS. Spencer could legally enter the house because he had the legal occupancy rights from the UEP Trust to that house. At once, the son called in the god squad, the FLDS security, and the city marshals.

The Mohave County deputies made sure the city marshals and the god squad didn't do something stupid. When this group arrived I felt secure knowing the Mohave County deputies would not put up with the FLDS baloney.

I stayed in the house with Spencer for about an hour talking to his under-aged daughters who had been brainwashed into believing their father was evil and that they should never be under his authority again.

Later, I went outside to join the rest of the family, his second wife, and their children. In a few minutes, all our cell phones went dead, except for the phones of the deputies. The god squad had a nifty little device that remotely shut down cell phones. Of course, this was illegal, but then again we were dealing with the FLDS, and what did illegal mean to them? One of the deputies let me use his phone to call Dawn and keep her up to date on what was happening. She then relayed the information to a prayer support team who were providing us with spiritual cover.

Spencer's oldest son was blocking his sisters from leaving. We told him that if he didn't cooperate we would see to it that he would be charged with kidnapping. The deputies informed the girls that since they were minors they needed to obey their father.

After about a four-hour standoff, the girls had their bags packed and finally got in the van with Spencer and the rest of the family. Later that afternoon, we all left town with a police escort for thirty miles to I-15. Once on I-15 safely headed north we were on our own.

I arrived home at about ten o'clock. I felt good about the day, but I also felt sad that I had not been with Michael on Sunday. Once again, I knew God had called me to that day's ministry and Dawn had to stand in the gap for me.

A couple of weeks later, Spencer called again. He told me the daughters had asked their father very politely if they would be allowed to sleep late the next morning and Spencer had agreed. The next morning at about eleven Spencer and his second wife, of their spiritual marriage, thought they better check the bedroom where all three girls were sleeping. They called for the girls, but there was no answer. They thought something seemed strange. The door was locked but they used a key to unlock the door. The window was open, the curtains were fluttering in the wind, and the girls were gone!

Spencer told me that around midnight he was awakened by what he thought was the sound of the vehicle's engine and a little bit of noise, but he dismissed it as a dream. After discovering the empty bedroom, they put two and two together and figured things out. Shortly after the girls arrived at their home they discovered the girls had a cell phone. Spencer had agreed to let the girls keep the phone if they behaved and would abide by the rules of the family. The girls had used their cell phones to make the escape plan.

They walked out to the road, and, sure enough, there were deep tire tracks on the shoulder of the road. The ground was soft because of the rain they had received the night before. The Clays realized that the FLDS had kidnapped the three minor girls. They also knew the girls were willing participants. By then they were eleven hours down the road and perhaps nearing one of the FLDS's compounds in South Dakota, Colorado, or on their way to the big new compound in Texas. Perhaps they would never be seen again.

One evening several months later, I got another phone call from Mr. Clay. The Idaho polygamist colony where he and his family relocated had been kind and welcoming to all of them for the first six months after their arrival. Then, one day everything changed.

There had been a freak accident at his work and Spencer had narrowly escaped getting killed. "This afternoon I was doing some digging project, working near a hole preparing for a new septic tank," he recounted, his voice shaking. "Only me and the local prophet were on the work site. The prophet was operating the back hoe that had an extended boom with a large digging bucket on the end. I came out of the hole and the machine was running full throttle when suddenly, out of the corner of my eye, I saw the boom swing toward me as fast as lightning. In a split second, I dropped back into the hole and the large steel bucket swung overhead. I had been within one or two seconds of being killed instantly! Mike, I think the prophet is trying to kill me. He wants me out of the way." I knew his intuition made sense.

Spencer went on to explain that if he was dead the prophet could take Spencer's youngest wife, a pretty young lady, as well as the young girls for himself. But there was a strange twist to it all. Spencer also told me that the prophet had taken a real liking to his three sons because they were outstanding workers. He explained that if he was killed it would be a win/win for the prophet. If Spencer was out of the picture the prophet also got his three sons as good workers. Then, in a few years, Spencer's young daughters, still children, would be physically mature enough for the prophet to take as wife material.

Spencer wanted someone to know that he thought he was in danger, in case they succeeded in killing him before he could make arrangements to get out of the cult. He asked me to tell my attorney friend, Ron, as well. I agreed to tell him the next day.

I knew the Clays needed to get out of the Idaho group. I immediately went back to Colorado City and helped Spencer negotiate a deal with the United Effort Plan Trust to get his house and shop back into his name so the family could get out of the Idaho polygamist group and move back to Colorado City. I put my reputation on the line with the leaders of the UEP Trust. Many in the community didn't like Spencer, but I stood with him.

We helped Spencer as much as we could, both financially and spiritually. God worked a miracle. The Trust issued a permit to get his house and shop back with an option to buy. We, along with Great Commission Utah and its supporters helped this family with thousands of dollars, part of which was a loan.

I walked life with Spencer and his family, gently teaching them spiritual truths. I also taught him that he should be sensitive to the issues that minorities live with every day. Many in the polygamist communities are very racist toward people of different skin colors. When I started working with Spencer I found that racism, especially against black people, was prevalent in his life. He had been taught a racist attitude from early childhood. At times it was very difficult working with the very people God had called me to work with.

Spencer said he had accepted Jesus as his personal Savior and was showing signs of spiritual growth. Several members of the Clay family had also come to accept Christ as their personal Savior. I held Bible studies with Spencer for about two years. Like so many who were hurt by the FLDS, they couldn't bring themselves to attend an organized Sunday worship service. Spencer decided to teach his family from the true Bible every evening.

One day, when I returned to Colorado City, I called Spencer to set up a time when we could get together. He declined to meet with me. His voice was cold and distant. I tried calling him many times, but he would not answer the phone. I finally just drove over to see if I could talk with him at his office. He made it very short, saying that I had talked behind his back to community leaders. A few in their community were opposed to my work and worked to drive a wedge between Spencer and me.

Later Spencer's second wife told one of our ministry leaders how badly she felt and how she appreciated all we had done for the family, but there was nothing she could do. Spencer defaulted on the loan. We discovered that was the way Spencer had treated most of his friends who had helped him along the way.

I struggled with what happened between Spencer and me. I asked myself at times if all my efforts had been worth it. I finally understood that I had to continue to work with those God called me to work with, I was, after all, His ambassador. I had to leave the results to God. I better understood the parable taught by Jesus in Matthew 13:1-9. The Parable of the Sower verses 5-6 says, "Other seeds fell on rocky ground, where they did not have much soil, and immediately they sprang up, since they had no depth of soil, but when the sun rose they were scorched. And since they had no root, they withered away." [ESV]

I planted seeds and I am not to judge Spencer. I am assured that his wife and some of the kids came to know the real Jesus as their Savior. Maybe in time the rest of the family will come to know Him. Only God knows. Again, I ask myself, *Was it worth it?* And the answer is a resounding *yes.* God calls us to be faithful to Him and His call on our lives. When God calls us to a task we are to respond to his marching orders and leave the results up to God. We are to be His ambassadors, humbling as it is at times.

Reflections & Pondering

Section 4

Chapters 9-12

So we are Christ's ambassadors; God is making his appeal through us. We speak for Christ when we plead, "Come back to God." 2 Corinthians 5:20 [NLT]

Reflections on <u>Your</u> Life

As you read the section "Spiritual Darkness" did any of these stories reflect on your own life?

In chapter 9, Mike quoted 1 John 5:4-5, "For every child of God defeats this evil world, and we achieve this victory through our faith, And who can win this battle against the world? Only those who believe that Jesus is the Son of God." [NLT] What does this verse mean to you?

Any thoughts or comments concerning the story of "The Dark House?"

When we see a closeup of the lives of ruthless people like the FLDS prophet, or in chapter 10 — the Somali military generals causing terrible turmoil and starvation, who is to blame?

How should we respond when we see these atrocities happening? Concerning chapter 11, what are your thoughts about Miriam, the mom, Big Mike the caretaker, Ruth, or Mike?

Mike and Ruth had to act quickly while listening to God. Any reflections from your life's past on listening to God during an emergency?

Regarding the Clay family, Mike stated that the ministry, Great Commission Utah, put more time, energy, and money into the Clay family than anyone else. In the end, Mr. Clay turned against him, or was it, "the end of the story? Was all that effort worth it? Why?

How does the Parable of the Sower, as recorded in Matthew 13:1-3, apply to this family? Does this story apply to you?

Do you have other questions or further comments about the stories in Chapters 9, 10, 11, or 12?

Pondering <u>Your</u> Life's Direction

Did anything in these chapters cause you to consider making a **Heart Change** in your life? If so, what was it that got you thinking?

Are there **Life Changes** you need to address as you mature as *an ambassador of Jesus*?

Section Five

God's Humor, Angels, and Ambassadorship

Thirteen

God's Sense of Humor

For not in my bow do I trust, nor can my sword save me.
But you have saved us from our foes
and have put to shame those who hate us.
Psalm 44:6-7 [ESV]

Don't **Take Your Guns To Town, Son.** "Mike, driving that red pick-up truck of yours around town irritates the FLDS. You know that, don't you? Have you ever thought about carrying a weapon when in The Crick? The FLDS don't like you. You know that, right?" One day at the Merry Wives Cafe, I heard these questions and more from my friend, an Arizona County Investigator.

The FLDS had banned the color red in CC/H. They taught that when Jesus returned to rule the world from Colorado City, Arizona, and Hildale, Utah he would wear a red robe. Therefore, the color red was banned from their community. Red was honored as holy. (The hilarious note is that Jeffs was wearing red shorts on the day he was arrested.)

I was being followed regularly by the FLDS god squad in their new, jacked-up, black 350 series Ford Trucks with illegal heavily tinted windows. This was their way of harassing me. They followed me, sometimes within a few feet of my rear bumper.

A few years prior, the FLDS Prophet, Warren Jeffs, had been captured and sent to prison in Texas. The FLDS leadership in Colorado City and the god squad were nervous and on edge. There was tension in the community. The trial of their "god-prophet" was coming up within months. Reporters from all over the country seemed to be swarming that little community of 12,000 people. The FBI agents were questioning many people in the community as well.

Earlier Jeffs had said that if it looked like the authorities would close in on him and the FLDS Church, the blood would flow down the streets of Colorado City. Therefore, some of those who knew me were getting increasingly concerned for my safety.

I wrestled with the issue of whether or not I should carry a concealed weapon. I shared my concerns with Dawn, hoping to get some traction to apply for a handgun permit. Dawn's response was unequivocal; "So, let me get this straight. You are a missionary to the people God called you to serve, to be an ambassador of Jesus, and to present them with the Good News of the Jesus of the Bible. On the other hand, you are ready to pull out your gun and blow them away." She made her point; no concealed weapons for me.

The next month I returned to my corner room in the log building. By now it was called the Community Center and was operated by Grace Reigns. Sleep wouldn't come to me that night and after an hour and a half of tossing and turning, I decided to get up and hit the road. I jumped into the clothes I had laid ready for the next day. My bag was packed. I left my room and walked toward the front door at the other end of the building and opened the door. I started down the steps when suddenly the lights of one of the god squad trucks snapped on, shining directly at me. I was a bit startled and shaken. *Should I have purchased that handgun?*

I calmly got into my red truck, locked the doors, and started the engine. I was shaking like a leaf. I took my usual route out of town and headed west toward Highway 359. The black F-350 truck stayed on my tail, almost on my bumper for several miles. It seemed like the god squad was getting braver in those days. Why had they been outside my door in the middle of the night? If they intended to intimidate me, they had succeeded.

All the way home I wondered, God called me to this work, but it sure seemed to be getting harder and harder. I decided I was not going to quit and give in to the devil or let his workers in this cult scare me into quitting. I had a plan. I didn't need a permit to carry if I took my 12-gauge shotgun with me the next time I returned to the Crick. My long gun was not considered a concealed weapon.

When I drove into town the next month, I gave the god squad ample time to know I was back. They had over a hundred cameras mounted in the twin towns, mostly on utility poles. The staff at the FLDS surveillance center knew every move people made and every non-community vehicle that entered the town. They had very sophisticated cameras on the three main entrances into the Crick. As usual, I rode slowly past the first camera and drove down Main Street on my way to the log building.

Three blocks after I entered the town the god squad had located me. They followed me to the log building and parked across the street. I parked directly in front of the log building. However, that time on my arrival, I did something a little differently. I stepped out of my red GMC truck and stretched. I stood there for a moment looking directly at the black truck. I tried to look cool and calm. I knew they were watching me from behind those heavily tinted windows. I reached behind the driver's seat of the club cab and pulled out my Winchester 12 gauge, pump-action shotgun – in its case. I removed it from the case for all to see. With the other hand, I reached back into the club cab and took out a box of 12 gauge shells. I pumped the action a couple of times, and, one at a time, placed the shells into the gun. Lastly, I put a shell into the chamber of the gun, and I checked the safety button. Next, I opened my suitcase and placed the box of shells inside, looked at the big black truck, smiled at the guys behind the blackened windows, and walked into the building.

When I got to my room I took the shells out of the gun, placed the gun back into its gun case, and set the shells on the window sill. That was the last time the god squad followed me.

For the next few visits, when I stayed in the log building, my home away from home, the last thing I did before bed was to take the shotgun out of its case, load it, put the safety switch to the "on" position, and put the gun on my nightstand beside me. I then jammed a chair under the door handle. After all, I was alone in that big old log building.

One night after several months of this routine, I went to bed as usual. I didn't think too much about the FLDS god squad thugs out there since by then they were pretty much leaving me alone. I fell asleep soon. I had finished a long day and was tired. At precisely two o'clock, I was suddenly awakened by the sound of what I thought was the activation of my truck alarm. Startled and shaking a bit, I jumped out of bed, pulled on my blue jeans, and slipped into my shoes. I grabbed my shotgun and slid the safety button to the "off" position. A shell was in the chamber and three more were in the tube.

Slowly, I opened my bedroom door and stepped into the main area. There was enough light coming from the windows that I could see where I was headed. When I got to the front door and the horn was still blasting away. I carefully opened the front door, gun in my hand, finger on the trigger, and ready to fire. But I stopped. Something wasn't right.

When the alarm goes off, the horn not only blares, but my vehicle lights also flash on and off. As I opened the door a little farther, I could hear the horn, but no lights were flashing. I carefully looked around and, to my astonishment, I realized it was not my truck alarm going off. It was the alarm of a truck down the street.

As I got back in bed I was rattled and pretty uneasy. If someone was messing with my truck would I have shot him? More questions kept me awake. If someone was trying to steal my truck or lure me outside and they were armed, what if they got the first shot?

The thoughts stuck with me all the next day and on into my nightly routine of loading the gun and resting it on the nightstand beside my bed. Almost always sleep comes easily to me and that night was no exception.

Right at two o'clock I awoke again. This time I had a vivid dream of Johnny Cash singing "Don't Take Your Guns to Town," a song that I hadn't heard in over twenty years. In the narrative of the song, a mother pleads with her son, who is about to embark on a journey west.

"Don't take your guns to town, son, Leave your guns at home, Bill ..."

Bill reassures her that he wouldn't "shoot without a cause," but his mom cries as he rides off into the distance. When he reaches a small "cattle town" he enters a bar with his mother's words echoing in his mind. After drinking heavily, a "dusty cowpoke" in the bar starts giving him a hard time. Again, Bill remembers his mom's words. But it is too late. Enraged, Bill reaches for his gun, but the cowpoke beats him to the draw and gets off the first shot. Even as Bill lay on the floor, blood draining from his chest, he remembered, slowly and faintly, repeating his mother's last words to him: "Don't take your guns to town, son ..."

That dream cut me to the core. I sat on the edge of my bed and figured it must have been a message from God. Yes, God speaks to his people by His word; Psalm 44:6-7a, "For not in my bow do I trust, nor can my sword save me. But you have saved us from our foes and have put to shame those who hate us." [ESV] And yes, God speaks to us through dreams as well. Johnny Cash became a Christian and long after he died, this man of God had a powerful warning for me. God works in mysterious ways.

I reached for that 12-gauge on the bed stand, unloaded it, put the shells back in the box, and the gun back in the case. I lay down and went to sleep. I called Dawn the next morning and told her about my dream. She laughed and agreed with the message. I never again took a defensive weapon with me on any return trips to the Crick.

Through a dream that night I learned a big lesson in my maturing as an ambassador of Jesus. I was maturing, nevertheless, God had much work to do in me, molding me into the person He wanted me to become.

***

Old Orange – If you would take a few moments and back up with me to the summer of 1975, I would like to share a story some have told me that I just simply needed to share in my autobiography. The story is about my dealings with an ex-con, an orange chair, and the FBI. It is a true story; sad in some ways, but hilarious in others.

You may ask the question, what does this story have to do with the central theme of *Ambassadors of Jesus*? My response to the question is simply; even ambassadors of Jesus receive mixed blessings!

It was late one Friday afternoon in July. I was 30 years old and was the newly elected state representative from Minnesota's 26-A District. About two weeks earlier Dawn and I had welcomed our second son, Michael Dale Menning, into our family.

I was in Luverne, Minnesota, about twenty-one miles from home. I stopped at a payphone and called home. Dawn was relieved that I had called. She informed me that Lon Morsley, my ex-con friend, had called to our home. He said he was coming through and wanted to stop at our house to pay us back for the $200 we had loaned him when he was released from the South Dakota State Penitentiary about a year earlier. I said I would hurry home as fast as my truck would take me. She breathed a sigh of relief and hoped I would get home before Mr. Morsley arrived. About fifteen minutes after I made it home, he arrived.

This story started about four years earlier when I became involved with a national ministry called "Man to Man" or for short, the M-2 program. The ministry's mission was to match a Christian guy with an inmate. My match was a guy named Lon Morsley. I visited Lon about twice a month. Later a prison official told me that Lon was a tough dude, but he had a history of showing loyalty to those who treated him right. Over a few years, he seemed to trust me and told me some about his past. He mentioned a former girlfriend who he wanted to visit when he got out. He even told me the name of the small town where she lived. I liked Lon, but for some reason when I got home after each visit, I scribbled a few notes in a file I had begun. I kept the notes in a manila folder. Each time I got back to the car after a visit, I developed a habit of writing on my notepad a few interesting parts of the conversation between Lon and me. It was just something I felt led to do, maybe it would be useful someday. Wow, little did I know that one day those notes would be useful to the FBI.

In a few more years Lon would be released from the South Dakota State Penitentiary. Upon release, he would be handed $65 by the state and sent on his way, not much for a new start in life after prison.

Time went on and I began enjoying my visits with Lon. I shared some of my joys and some of my hurts. I remember one day Lon asked me the question, "Mike, how are you doing? I mean really what's going on? You seem to be troubled."

I told him that I was in the process of selling my Foresight Distribution business to a guy from Omaha. I explained to him that we made the deal and shook hands on it. We had an appointment arranged at the bank for the following morning at which time we would officially close on the business deal, and then I would be paid in full. The evening before our appointment he asked if he could study my customer list overnight so he would be ready to roll immediately after he became the new owner. I made a serious mistake and gave him the list. I told Lon that I trusted this guy when I shouldn't have. This prospective buyer made a copy of the customer's profiles and backed out of the deal the next morning. A few days later I found out that he was calling on all my customers using the inside information he had stolen from me!

As I mentioned earlier, the prison officials told me that Lon was known to be fiercely loyal to his friends on the outside. I found out what they meant. Lon asked me if he could get involved in a little justice for the Omaha guy. I was naive and said I didn't know what he meant. He said, "Mike, this guy messed with you, my friend. Give me his name and address and I can get a friend on the outside to burn him out – his business, and his home."

I nearly jumped out of my skin, I said, "Lon, no, no, Lon, I don't want anything to do with that."

Lon said, "Well if you ever change your mind, I'll put out the word." I learned another lesson that day - be careful telling too much to people I don't know well.

At the end of serving his prison time, Lon was released. I was there to pick him up at the gate. Dawn and I purchased a new set of clothes for him – a leisure suit, socks, and shoes – the works. Lon and I drove a couple of miles from the Penitentiary to the Sioux Falls Airport. He changed out of his prison-issued clothing at the airport. He was looking pretty sharp, and he had $265 in his pocket. The money consisted of $65 from the state and a $200 loan from the Mennings. Lon caught a flight to Flint, Michigan. His last words to me were, "Mike, I'll pay the money back to you."

We did get two cards in the mail – one a Mother's Day card for Dawn that included a sweet message, and another "thinking of you" card. Neither had a return address and I guess we didn't pay too much attention to the canceled postmark.

And then on that hot and humid July afternoon, it happened. Lon Morsley had called our home and told Dawn he was on his way to our house. Lon drove up to our home in a spanking new Chevrolet Monte Carlo. I went outside and was greeted with a big hug from my former M-2 buddy. I noticed the back end of the car was hanging low and the back seat was full up to the windows of something covered with a black tarp.

We stood outside for a few minutes exchanging niceties and soon stepped into the house. Dawn was holding our two-week-old baby. Lon said it was great to be in our home. We had some afternoon coffee and a snack. Lon asked if I could give him a tour of a farming operation, so I took him to my brother Art's dairy farm. After a little bit, Lon seemed to be a bit nervous and said he was in kind of a hurry and needed to get back on the road. We went back to our home. He handed me $200, two new crisp one-hundred-dollar bills. His loan was paid in full and he was on his way.

Earlier that week we had shopped at the Big Red Barn, also known as Vander Stoep Furniture in our hometown of Edgerton, Minnesota. We eyed a beautiful orange La-Z-Boy recliner – what a treasure for a mommy who nursed her baby! It was sharp-looking, comfortable, orange, and very expensive for 1975 – $189.

Lon was no more than out of sight and we decided to head over to the Big Red Barn and purchase the orange La-Z-Boy recliner. We paid for it with two crisp one-hundred-dollar bills. We proudly brought our new purchase home in my truck.

That evening we took turns sitting on our orange La-Z-Boy recliner and I must add, it was a very comfortable La-Z-Boy. I couldn't believe it -- we owned a La-Z-Boy recliner! It was a little light outside around nine o'clock that evening when the local Deputy Sheriff Pool pulled into our driveway with his cruiser. I knew him well, he was the same deputy who had provided us with a police escort out of town on our wedding night. I said to Dawn, "I wonder what he wants?" He got out of the car and rang the doorbell. I went to greet him and invited him in.

Mr. Marion Pool's nickname was "Mutt." He was a great guy – I will say I am glad that although I shared his surname, I never got that nickname! He seemed a little more concerned than usual. He said, "Say, Mike and Dawn, I don't want to worry you, but I just got a call from an FBI agent in the Sioux Falls office. He said, "'The FBI has information that a former prisoner you visited through the M-2 program at the state penitentiary, Lon Morsley is now wanted for a crime and is on the run.'"

He went on to tell us, "The information pointed to the fact that you were his only friend on the outside listed on his prison record. Furthermore, they said he was traveling this way, and he may want to stop in to look you up." Before I could get a word in edgewise, he said, "If he stops in, please don't try to be a hero. Just let him talk and act as if you don't know anything. Then when he is gone, you give me a call."

I was finally able to say, "Well, Mutt, I'll tell you what, you missed Lon Morsley by four hours. He left here about four hours ago." Mutt got pretty wide-eyed. I told him that he had paid us back the $200 that he owed me and that we just returned from Vander Stoep Furniture with our new orange La-Z-Boy recliner, paid for with two crisp one-hundred-dollar bills."

Mutt said, "Who knows? Maybe he stole the money."

I said, "Yeah, the money may have been hot. But this orange La-Z-Boy recliner surely is comfortable to sit in. Come on Mutt, have a seat and try it out." I further chided him a little and asked if he wanted to take the chair along. He chuckled and said he had to get going. That was Saturday evening.

Sunday afternoon Mutt pulled into the driveway again. This time he informed me that since I was heading back to the capitol in St. Paul on Monday morning, the FBI of Minneapolis/St. Paul wanted to further question me.

I arrived at my office on Monday morning and my secretary

Marge seemed shaken. She immediately informed me that two FBI agents were waiting in my office and said they wanted to talk to me. I assured her that everything was alright and that I had some information they were looking for. I entered my office and was pleased to present the file I had kept on Mr. Morsley. I showed them the name of Lon's girlfriend and the name of the small town and state where she lived. They had some other questions and were happy with the information I had provided them.

I told them the whole story, from a description of the car he was driving, about the back seat filled with something, the cover over whatever it was, and that Lon had paid me back the $200 I had loaned him the day of his release. They informed me that Lon had stolen that new Monte Carlo, robbed a bank in Alabama, and drove to Rapid City, South Dakota, where he picked up machine guns and hand grenades. He left Rapid City, drove nearly 400 miles east, and stopped to see the guy who faithfully visited him while in prison (that was me)!! They figured he planned to head southeast from my place to deliver his goods.

A few weeks passed before Deputy Marion Pool drove back into my driveway. He reported that Lon Morsley was captured at his former girlfriend's place and was safely back in prison. Mr. Pool also said the FBI was appreciative of the file folder I presented to them. Mutt said, "You had recorded the information about Lon's girlfriend and where she lived, and that is where they arrested him and his girlfriend."

As for Old Orange which we had purchased with two crisp one-hundred-dollar bills fresh out of a bank robbery in Alabama, I told the FBI that they could have the orange chair if they returned it to the bank in Alabama. Or, if the bank would pay for the shipping, I would send the chair to them. They passed on the idea and told us to enjoy the La-Z-Boy.

The orange La-Z-Boy recliner was enjoyed (for almost 45 years) by our family from 1975 until about 2019. We named the chair "Old

Orange." It went with us from our honeymoon house in Edgerton to the acreage north of town. Minnesota Governor Wendell R. Anderson, Governor Rudy Perpich, Congressman Rick Nolan, and many others sat in Old Orange. Later we took Old Orange with us when we moved to our new home in Rock Valley, Iowa. In 2000 Republican Candidate for President, Lamar Alexander took a rest in the chair as well. Then, Old Orange came with us to our home in Salt Lake City. It moved on to the next generation. Our son Mitch and his wife Kara enjoyed Old Orange in their nursery for several years. It later moved to their downstairs family room.

I think the year was 2019 when I loaded Old Orange into the back of my 1999 Red Chevy narrow box truck and carefully brought Old Orange to the Thrift Store in the polygamist town of Colorado City, Arizona. Much to our surprise, Pastor Brody Olson and his wife, Liz, our very special friends living in Colorado City purchased Old Orange for a few bucks. The special chair now holds a prominent spot in their 1000-square-foot living room in their former polygamist house. It is once again being put to good use and get this – the color orange has come back into style.

As for Old Orange, she is looking good, almost like new, and continues to be a part of my life! In my ministry of walking life and mentoring many former polygamists of this town, I traveled to Colorado City once a month for the past ten years or more. In the last couple of years when I stayed with the Olsons, my home away from home, I've been reunited with Old Orange. Now that I am retired, I get to see Old Orange and sit in the comfort of that great, old La-Z-Boy a couple of times a year. Our dear friends, the Olsons, told me that after I am gone, Old Orange will live on since they plan to pass Old Orange on to the next generation.

Fourteen

Angels Watching Over Me

*The time came when the beggar died
and the ANGELS carried him to Abraham's side.
Luke 16:22[NIV]*

I have always looked forward to a good road trip with our family. We anticipated, with joy and excitement, the thrill of traveling to new places we had not seen or experienced. In our 55 plus years of marriage, most often Dawn researched the potential stopping places we could see along the way before we arrived at the much-anticipated vacation destination. The possibilities of stops along the way, sights to see, and experiences that were awaiting us created excitement in each of us.

For years Mitch, having some of the same gifts as his mother, helped Dawn in this area and he started the tradition later in his own family. Isaiah, our oldest grandson, also has this gift.

The anticipated journey was part of the overall vacation. When it was time to go home, however, Dawn said that I was like "a horse headed for the barn." Don't stop, just keep moving.

The exhilaration of riding a horse to a certain destination and then feeling your horse's excitement when he heads for home is an experience that only a horse's rider can understand. I vividly remember my horse Buckshot turning on a dime when he knew it was time to go home. I just let him go as fast as he wanted and it seemed as though his hooves barely touched the ground. Oh my, he didn't slow down very much when he left the ditch and turned into the driveway, heading into the farmyard. He missed the corner post by an inch or two. Old Buckshot was like a motorcyclist leaning into a fast turn.

There is something special about going home. Some find it a little strange, but it seems the older I get the more I look forward to my heavenly home.

While I served on the Board of Directors for Joni and Friends, I began to gain a special interest in heaven and all we can know about our eternal home. There were many times that my friend Joni and I just sat and talked about heaven. With great excitement, we dreamed about what heaven would be like and about the trip getting there.

I find it interesting that people love to think about going on long trips; they plan and dream about what it will be like. However, studies have shown that few people like to think about *heaven* and what it's going to be like. For me, it is the most exciting thing I can talk about. There are times when I bring up the topic, and some people give me a very puzzled look.

The apostle Paul said in 2 Corinthians 5:8, "We are confident, I say, and would prefer to be away from the body and at home with the Lord." [NIV]

I would rather be with the Lord, absent from my "wearing-out" body as well. On the other hand, I certainly want to be with my family for now. I am concerned for Michael and pray that I can see the day that God carries him home where he will be healed and free, no longer a prisoner in his mind and body. My prayer is also that I can do for the Lord all that He has planned for me to do before I go home. I pray that I can see my grandkids through high school age, and be a blessing to them on their life journey. If God answers my prayers in the affirmative, I will live well into my 80s.

I know, with all certainty and as surely as the sun will go down tonight, that one day I will head home. I am very excited about planning for my trip to heaven, thinking and dreaming of what it will be like. I think a lot about paradise, the new heaven, and the new earth. I know, without a doubt, that when my work here is done I will be with the Lord.

Only my physical body will die, the real me will just depart from this broken body of flesh and bones as Psalm 90:10 says, "even the best years are filled with pain and trouble; soon they disappear, and we fly away." [NLT] The Bible refers to our bodies as the tents in which we formerly lived. 2 Corinthians 5:1 says, "For we know that if the tent that is our earthly home is destroyed, we have a building from God, a house not made with hands, eternal in the heavens." [ESV]

I am thrilled because the day is coming when I will get to meet Jesus face to face and talk with him. I will meet the Father and the Holy Spirit. I will meet characters from the Bible who were saved. I will meet my family who have gone before me. I look forward to joining all other believers at that moment.

I think perhaps I (and maybe all believers) will be escorted by angels to paradise, as Jesus said to the criminal on the cross, "Today you will be with me in paradise." Then on that great day when Jesus returns, the Bible says, we will live in that New Heaven and New Earth for all eternity! 2 Peter 3:7-13, Isaiah 65:17, and Isaiah 66:22 tell us that this present world will be destroyed by fire and there will be a new heaven and new earth. The Apostle John says in his vision, recorded in Revelation 21:1 "Then I saw "a new heaven and a new earth," for the first heaven and the first earth had passed away ..."

Luke 16:22 says, "The time came when the beggar died and the ANGELS carried him to Abraham's side. The rich man also died and was buried. In hell, where he was in torment, he looked up and saw Abraham far away, with Lazarus by his side. So he called to him,

Father Abraham, have pity on me and send Lazarus to dip the tip of his finger in water and cool my tongue because I am in agony in this fire," [NIV.] I interpret this verse to mean angels carry us to heaven. I believe the trip could be different for everyone.

My brother Johnnie, who was two years older than I, died of cancer when he was 49 years old. He spent his last days at Sioux Valley Hospital in Sioux Falls. The Sioux Falls Airport was our regional airport and I flew in and out of that airport regularly. One night I had a late flight coming back from a ministry trip to Grand Rapids, Michigan. I landed at 11:30 p.m. and knew Johnnie was in his last days here on earth. Shortly after midnight, I stopped at the hospital and walked into his room. It looked like he was sleeping so I thought I would let him sleep and not bother him. As I turned from his bed, he said, "Marion, don't leave, I was just thinking."

That night, at a little past midnight, Johnnie asked me if I believed that angels ever come to visit people in today's world. I said, "Yes, I do, I believe those types of visits are unusual, but certainly can and do happen."

Hesitantly at first, Johnnie went on to tell me a very unusual story that happened the night before, around two or three in the morning. The Sioux Valley Hospital (now called the Sanford Hospital) had very large windows in each room, taking the space of almost the entire outside wall. Johnnie told me that as he was lying in his hospital bed looking out the window into the darkness, contemplating his death, when he suddenly saw a bright light in the sky. He noticed there was something different about this light. He focused on the light and as he did, the light grew brighter and larger and seemed to be traveling at a high speed, heading straight for the window in his room. As it got closer, he saw it was a horse with riders on its back. He said the riders were unmistakably angels and there were three or four on the horse's back.

He shared what he heard, "Johnnie," the angel spoke to him, "we will be back to take you with us soon. There is no room on the horse right now, but we will be back very soon."

It was about forty-eight hours later that Johnnie left the tent he lived in. Without a doubt, I believe that the angels kept their word and escorted my brother to heaven.

Marvin Besteman's book "My Journey to Heaven," tells of his near-death experience, and was written by Lorilee Craker and Marv. He described his trip to heaven this way, in the introduction of the book. "Suddenly, two men I had never seen before in my life walked into my hospital room. Don't ask me how I knew, but immediately I had the sense that these men were angels. I wasn't the least bit anxious, either.

Once they had detached me from my tangle of tubes, the angels gathered me in their arms and we began to ascend, on a quick journey. It felt light and smooth through the bluest of blue skies."[1]

Yes, Marvin was escorted by angels.

Later in the book, Marvin said he was told that he had to return from the gates of heaven back to his life on earth. He explained that his trip back was different. He said he was suddenly transformed back into his hospital bed and experienced the pain just as before he left to spend a glimpse into heaven.

A few years ago I had a conversation with Don Piper, author of "90 Minutes in Heaven." I asked him about his trip to heaven. I refer to the two opening paragraphs of chapter 2 in his book to share his answer: "When I died, I didn't flow through a long, dark tunnel. I had no sense of fading away or of coming back. I never felt my body being transported into the light. I heard no voices calling to me or anything else. Simultaneous with my last recollection of seeing the bridge, a light enveloped me, with a brilliance beyond earthly comprehension or description. Only in my next moment of awareness, I was standing in heaven."[1] Don Piper didn't see any angels and didn't experience a trip to heaven.

Charles Spurgeon was without a doubt one of the greatest and most well-respected preachers of his time. His work and teachings are respected to this day. His right-hand man and maybe best friend Joseph Harrald was with Spurgeon when he died. He insisted that at Spurgeon's death, God opened his eyes and he saw hosts of angels above the hills of Menton, France, where Spurgeon died.

I think that for those who die, the Lord takes them from this world into the next in different ways. I believe that many angels are sent by God to care for His people. One of the reasons I believe it to be true is because it says this in the Bible. Matthew 18:10, Jesus says, "See that you do not despise one of these little ones. For I tell you that **their** angels in heaven always see the face of my Father in heaven," [NIV]

In the first chapter of this book, I told the story of an angel visiting me during the time I was running for my party's nomination for governor in Minnesota.

I want to tell you another story of two angels visiting me when I was shaking in my boots on my way to deliver an important document to the CEO of Intermountain Health Care System. The document reports an unfortunate incident following Dawn's surgery on March 3, 2017. The full story can be read in the United States Congressional Record of December 12, 2018, as entered by Minnesota Congressman Richard Nolan.

The time was 9:30 a.m. Wednesday, December 13, 2017. I was headed north on I-15 and my destination was the downtown Salt Lake City office of Dr. A. Mark Harrison, the CEO of Intermountain Health Center (IHC), a mammoth organization that employed 34,000 people. I intended to hand-deliver a letter I wrote to Dr. Harrison. The letter contained the description of my wife, Dawn, being dropped off the operating table at the Intermountain Medical Hospital on the morning of March 3, 2017. It also contained a description of how poorly the IHC attorney treated us. I hoped that if I couldn't see Dr. Harrison personally, I could give it to his secretary.

I spent much time in prayer before what most people would consider one of the craziest things I have ever done. I was convinced God placed it on my heart to hand deliver the letter.

Dawn had edited the letter and I knew it was in good shape. As I was going down the highway in early morning traffic, a dark feeling of fear came over me. It seemed as if an evil spirit was speaking to me. "Who do you think you are doing this? Anyone in their right mind knows that the CEO of the largest business in Utah will have security around him like no one else in the state. There is no way you can even get close to his office."

Dr. Harrison led a corporation with the largest number of employees in one organization in the State of Utah. I had figured out from the letter I received from one of the IHC attorneys that his office was on the 24th floor of their downtown corporate office building. My gut was churning and my heart began to pound at the thought of actually carrying out my mission.

That morning, I dressed differently than I usually do. I knew no one around that office would be dressed as I was. I wore western-style clothes, my $4 western boots that I had picked up at the Common Grounds Thrift Store in The Crick two weeks before, my leather jacket, and blue jeans. I wanted to stick out like a sore thumb, for sure security would immediately notice me; but I knew if it truly was of God, HE would pull me through.

As I was getting closer, my faith was withering quickly and my stomach was churning. I prayed, almost in a panic, *Lord, was that you working in my heart? Was that your voice I heard or was it an evil spirit disguised as an angel of light? Should I be doing this crazy thing? Was I hearing you correctly? Should I have worn different clothes? I've never been in this building and I am sure there are guards everywhere who will see me dressed as I am.*

Suddenly, the Lord felt very near. A calmness flowed over me like a warm bath; God's words washed over me like water. *"I will open the way for you. Don't be afraid. I am with you."*

It was as if He was sitting right there with me in my truck. I played those words over and over in my mind.

The 600 South exit appeared quickly and I headed into downtown Salt Lake. A couple of miles later, I found myself driving my red pickup truck into the parking lot beneath the office building at 36 S. State Street, the headquarters of IHC.

The Lord's message continued running through my mind. *I will open the way for you. Don't be afraid. I am with you.* Even so, my stomach cramps got worse. I parked my red truck and headed toward the main lobby believing God was with me. Sure enough, all the men were wearing dress suits, freshly pressed shirts, and ties. Yes, I stuck out like a sore thumb!

The sign above the elevators read "To the 14th Floor." I knew what that meant. On the 14th floor, there would be another set of secured elevators that would go to the next levels of the building. There would be a guard posted near those elevators who would check identification before allowing anyone to go to higher floors. *I will open the way for you. Don't be afraid. I am with you.*

I got on another elevator and rode to the 14th floor. I stepped off the elevator, went around to the backside, and spotted a guard walking away from his desk to talk to someone. I heard him say, "I have to step away for a second. I'll be right back."

I got on the elevator and ascended as high as the 21st floor. I got off the elevator and looked around. *I will open the way for you. Don't be afraid. I am with you.*

Only a few people were milling around. "Can I help you?" a gentleman in a suit asked me. "Who are you looking for?" My heart skipped a beat. Would he report me to the guard?

I told the truth. "I am looking for Dr. Harrison's office and have a letter to deliver to him."

He looked around. "Oh, the guard must have left for a minute or two. Come with me."

We went around the backside to another set of elevators. I stepped into the elevator and pushed the button for floor 24.

I imagined there would be clear glass doors going into the VIP section on the 24th floor with a guard behind the desk on the other side of the locked doors. The elevator stopped, the doors opened and there were the big glass doors. A rush of people emerged from the doors that I assumed would lead to the office of Dr. Harrison. I held the glass door open for all the people to pass by as they left. When the people were out I held the glass door open with my foot.

The elevator door across from me stayed open for what seemed like a longer-than-usual time. There were about ten people in the elevator.

Then the most peculiar thing happened. One of the guys in the middle of the back row of the elevator motioned to me. I distinctly remember him, yet I find it impossible to describe him. He was wearing clothes different from the others, but I can't tell you exactly what they looked like. He had on a sport coat with a very bright shirt of an unusual color. It seemed like it was red, but it wasn't red like I knew red to be.

He motioned for me to pass through the glass door I was holding open with my foot. The others didn't seem to notice him. He smiled and continued to motion with his hand. He was trying to make it clear that he wanted me to walk through the open glass door. The others in the elevator were oblivious to me standing there holding the door open and they didn't notice the guy saying to me, "Go ahead, walk in!" The man smiled and spoke in a crisp, clear, loud voice.

I didn't understand what was happening at the moment, but I took the stranger's advice and walked through the open glass doors.

At that moment I think God was looking down on me with a smile or maybe He was "singing over me" as Zephaniah 3:17 says.

The guard who should have been behind the security desk in this heavily guarded corporation headquarters was nowhere to be seen. This was the third guard station where the guards were simply not at their stations! God cleared the way for me.

I realized then that the guy who had motioned for me to go inside must have been an angel sent by God. *I will open the way for you. Don't be afraid. I am with you.* Surely it was true. God sent his angel to show me the way and encourage me. The jitters were gone!

I had cleared every obstacle and was standing in one of the most secure parts of one of the most secure buildings in all of Utah.

Time seemed to stand still. From the empty desk of the guard, there were three hallways, one turned right, one turned left, and one headed straight ahead in a northerly direction. I was alone, or so I thought.

I started to walk down the hallway to the right. Suddenly, out of nowhere, a young man was at my side. Walking beside me, he asked, "Can I help you?"

He was totally "dressed down" compared to the corporate world. He was a couple of inches shorter than I and had fine features. He was wearing a bulky sweater and his sleeves were pulled up just above the wrists. The sweater seemed a little too big. It was also a color I had never seen before, appearing to be somewhere between red, yellow, orange, and pink! The colors were mixed, yet separate. That's the best I can describe. I had never seen it before, similar to the unusual reddish color worn by the man in the elevator. Those new-to-me colors were amazingly awesome.

"Who are you looking for?" The young man asked.

"I am looking for Dr. Harrison's office," I replied.

"Oh, his office is just down the hall. Follow me."

We walked down the hall and he pointed. "This is Dr. Harrison's office."

I looked and there was a large office, in the southeast corner of the building. The hallway wall in front of the office was made of glass and so was the door.

I recognized Dr. Harrison from pictures on the internet when I was researching IHC. Through the glass walls, I saw Dr. Harrison come out of his office. He greeted someone, talked to him, and invited him into his office. The office door was open. "Dr. Harrison," I said in a loud voice. But it was as though I was invisible. No one turned when I spoke. It seemed as if they didn't hear or see me. I stood there and again I called out, "Dr. Harrison." Again, no one noticed me. I turned to the young man in the multicolored sweater, but he had vanished.

Dr. Harrison had not heard me. He invited the other man into his private office. Then I saw four desks occupied by three secretaries. I approached the secretary nearest to me and introduced myself. She was very kind and receptive.

She listened intently as I told the story of how Dawn had been dropped from the operating table. I choked up when I told the story. I shared how the hospital management team had treated us. I explained that the first attorney had treated me like trash. By this time, the receptionist was crying. I asked if she would be so kind as to give the full packet of information and the letter to Dr. Harrison. With tears running down her cheeks, she said she was so sorry for what we had been through. She agreed to give Dr. Harrison the full package.

As I headed from Dr. Harrison's office I walked down the hallway where I had entered. I saw the guard now sitting at his desk and he glared at me. I was not wearing a visitor's badge and it seemed as if he saw me for the first time. He must have been thinking, *Did I mess up? I have never seen this guy before. Will I be in trouble? I did not issue this guy a visitor's badge. How did he get in here and what has he been doing here?*

As I passed his desk I smiled at him, opened the big glass door, and walked out into the elevator area. Once again, I was standing in front of the elevator which would take me down to the 21st floor. I entered the next elevator, facing the open door. That guard's eyes seemed like a laser burning right through me. However, I was no longer afraid and my stomach was calm! I smiled, nodded, and gave the guard a little wave of the hand as the elevator door closed.

I marveled as I left Dr. Harrison's office complex. I had been encouraged by the first angel to move forward from the crowded elevator, and then an angel in a multi-colored sweater escorted me to Dr. Harrison's office. It was over. God's promise was kept. *I will open the way for you. Don't be afraid. I am with you.*

Oh, yes, I believe angels come to earth to care for God's people, and at times we get to see them!

Fifteen

My Ambassadorship

We are therefore Christ's ambassadors,
as though God were making his appeal through us.
2 Corinthians 5:20a [NIV]

One summer day after I graduated from high school, a seed of compassion for the lost was planted in my spirit.

We needed some supplies for the farm and the only place they were available was in Sioux Falls, South Dakota, a 110-mile round trip from our farm. I felt so close to the Lord while driving there, I thought about how Jesus had saved me from my sins, and then my thoughts turned to people who didn't know Jesus. These thoughts began to consume me. If those people died without knowing Him, they would be lost forever. What could I do about it?

On my return trip as I headed east on Interstate 90, I saw many cars on the road. Again, I wondered how many people in those vehicles knew Jesus as their personal Savior. Tears rolled down my cheeks as I drove home.

Until that time, I had talked about spiritual matters to my parents only a few times, if ever. Sometimes we talked of religion, but in those days, our relationship with Jesus was not brought up.

When I came home that day and walked into the house, my mother could see that I had been crying. She and I were alone in that old broken-down farmhouse. She asked me what was wrong. "Oh, nothing," I answered quickly.

"Is everything okay between you and Dawn? There's no problem, is there?"

Suddenly I broke down and wept. I told her what struck me that day. She was shocked and didn't know how to respond. However, I saw a real sense of caring in her eyes about what I had experienced that day.

"I think you should become a minister," she said a bit later. Becoming a minister – as was said in those days – was the farthest thing from my mind, yet my yearning for the lost never left me. God planted "a seed of compassion" in my heart that day. At that time, I believed a person had to be a pastor to lead people to Christ. Little did I realize, what is impossible with man is possible with God.

Jumping forward a few years, while I was serving in the legislature, my fellow Christian legislator friends and a couple of pastors taught me how to invite someone to trust in Christ. I realized for the first time that I didn't have to be a pastor to lead others to Jesus. All along, God was preparing me to be an ambassador of Jesus.

At age thirty-one, I became a Minnesota State Senator and had my first experience leading someone into a saving relationship with Christ. One night I attended a meeting in the Minneapolis/St. Paul area. A staff person of a fellow senator was also at the gathering and needed a ride back to the capitol where his car was parked. On our way back to the State Capitol Building, Mark and I talked about spiritual matters.

I remember parking the car in front of the capitol at about 10:00 when Mark asked me how he could accept Jesus. I had my Bible in my briefcase. I was shaking like a leaf, trying to remember what verses to read with him. Right there in my car, I led him through the sinner's prayer. He confessed his sins and told God that he believed Jesus was the Son of God, and that he desired to serve Him for the rest of his life. Mark is faithfully serving the Lord to this day.

As I look back, I realize I don't have any idea how many people I have led to Jesus over the years, and it doesn't matter. I don't keep track.

When God created mankind He was looking forward to His relationship with those He created. Jesus said that we can have a relationship with Him if we accept Him, just as He has a relationship with the Father. He created us so we can have Christ-like fellowship with other believers and with God.

It's amazing to me that the Son of God left heaven where He was with the Father and came down to earth to become fully God and fully man. He gave His perfect life to save His people from their sins as a free gift of salvation. Ephesians 2:8-9 says, "For it is by grace you have been saved, through faith—and this is not from yourselves, it is the gift of God— not by works so that no one can boast." [NIV]

God gives us spiritual gifts when we accept Jesus as our Savior. One of my gifts is evangelism which is leading others to Christ. Jesus deserves to have people know of the knowledge of salvation because of what He did on the cross. It is the free gift offered to all who confess their sin and believe He is the only Son of God. Only then can they receive eternal life - and receive their own spiritual gifts. I must use this gift to bring people to join the family of God here on Earth and for eternity. I received this as God's desired will for my life - that is what an ambassador of Jesus must do.

Once I attended a conference of the Christian Reformed Church promoting mission support and the need for more missionaries to reach the people of the world for Christ. The speaker, Mrs. Vanderaa, the wife of a missionary, based her message on Isaiah 6:8, "Then I heard the voice of the Lord saying, 'Whom shall I send? And who will go for us?' And I said, 'Here am I. Send me!'" [NIV] I bowed my head right then and there and quietly prayed, "Here am I, Lord, send me, wherever You wish, I will go where you want me to go, I will do what you want me to do. I trust you completely." God sent me, He equipped me, and He opened many doors for me.

The Great Commission compelled me to carry out my ambassadorship. "Then Jesus came to them and said, `All authority in heaven and on earth has been given to me. Therefore, go and make disciples of all nations (better-translated people groups), baptizing them in the name of the Father and of the Son and the Holy Spirit, and teaching them to obey everything I have commanded you. And surely I am with you always, to the very end of the age.'" Matthew 28:18-20 [NIV]

***

Part of my work with CRWRC included traveling through Oklahoma City on my way to visit churches in Texas. There was one guy from my high school class who lived in Oklahoma City, Wayne Kruen, who I think could be referred to as "Mr. Cool." He was raised in a Christ-centered home. When Wayne was in elementary school his mother died of Spino-cerebral Ataxia, known as Schuts Disease or Ataxia. Wayne knew it could be passed on to future generations.

I am guessing it was about twenty years after high school when he started to show symptoms of the disease. He knew there was no cure for Ataxia and that he too would have to travel the awful road his mother had traveled before she was taken from this earth. Wayne knew his years on earth were limited.

For a while, Wayne's older brother Carl kept me updated on Wayne's condition. I made plans to see Wayne on my way to Texas for a ministry trip. I understood that he was becoming more and more disabled. He had heard the truth of the Gospel hundreds of times being raised by strong Christian parents and educated in a Christian school and church.

Wayne did not show signs of being a Christ follower. I visited him two or three times in the next couple of years. Without a doubt God put in my heart that I needed to establish a relationship with him and walk life with him. I needed to dig deeper concerning his relationship with the Lord. I always had such a good time with him. We never failed to have some good belly laughs. But, there was something I needed to do. The Lord was nudging me. *You need to ask him the question, don't be afraid.*

"Wayne, where are you with the Lord?" I started a bit shaky. "Have you prayed to give your life to Jesus? Are you okay with Him?"

"Ya' know Mike, I have lived a good life. I never once cheated anyone out of anything. I saw my mother die of this horrible disease. I have lived a good life, I've been good to my wife and kids."

He then looked at me in all seriousness with a little side grin. "Ya' know, when I get to heaven's gate and meet St. Peter, I will make my case. When he reviews my life I don't think he will turn me away." Then he added his unique chuckle. "I think I'll slip in, just under the wire."

"Wayne, that all sounds good and, at first glance, even seems to make sense. You believe the Bible, don't you?"

"Very definitely."

I went on to share a few passages, one of which was Romans 10:9, "If you confess with your mouth, 'Jesus is Lord,' and believe in your heart that God raised him from the dead, you will be saved. One believes with the heart, resulting in righteousness, and one confesses with the mouth, resulting in salvation." [CSB] I had to say more, "Wayne, it's not St. Peter's decision."

Wayne didn't respond to my comments, but I could tell he was thinking about it.

On my last visit with him in Oklahoma City, he said he needed to get closer to family and back to his roots. Carl and Julie, Wayne's brother and sister-in-law were looking for a small apartment for him in Pipestone, Minnesota where they lived. At the time Dawn and I lived in Edgerton, just eighteen miles down the road from Pipestone.

Within a few months, Wayne moved to Pipestone. As soon as he arrived, I called him, asked if I could pick up a couple of Hardee's burgers, and suggested we have lunch together. He was excited and so was I. For the next couple of years, we regularly had good times together, eating burgers and talking.

Wayne was easy to talk with and one of the most positive people I have ever met. There was always a smile on his face. It was impossible not to like the guy. We were both blessed.

One day, as I was leaving, heading out the door, he said with a shaky voice, "Hey, Mike, aren't you forgetting something."

"What's that?"

"Mike, we haven't prayed."

I was embarrassed, but his question was a good sign; I could see a glimmer of hope. Wayne was changing on the inside.

I told Wayne that our family was preparing to leave on a two-week vacation to Banff, Canada. I wished him well and said I planned to see him when I returned.

I received a call from his brother Carl the next day. Carl informed me that he checked Wayne into the local hospital and he was not doing well. Although we planned to leave the next day for our vacation, I knew I needed to see Wayne before we left. So I jumped in my car and headed for the hospital.

I was a little surprised to see my old friend lying in the hospital bed with oxygen attached. Wayne told me he was glad I was there and spoke with all the effort he had. "Mike, I need what you have."

"What do you mean?"

Wayne took a deep breath gathering as much strength as he could. "Oh, Mike, you know I need to have Jesus."

I asked if he wanted to pray to receive Jesus right then.

"Yes."

I had my Bible with me and I read the Romans 10:9-10 passage again. "Can you help me?" I took his hand and we prayed what some call "the sinner's prayer." Wayne prayed with all his heart.

I cry as I recall that moment and the smile he gave me. Then something happened that I had never seen before and have not seen since. Suddenly, there was a glow around Wayne's face. I can't tell you if it was over his whole body or not, but his face glowed with the most beautiful light I've ever seen. We talked a little more and though Wayne was exhausted, his countenance had peace. It was a peace that surpasses understanding. I stayed with him for a while longer, but he kept dozing off.

The glow remained. I knew the angels in heaven were rejoicing and I knew, with certainty, that the Holy Spirit had entered my old friend. I saw the glow with my own eyes. He told me he couldn't stay awake any longer. I said goodbye and that I hoped to see him when I returned from vacation. I walked out of that room feeling held by a loving God. I experienced spiritual peace and joy, rejoicing that Wayne was bound for heaven to be with Jesus for all eternity.

I went home excited and couldn't wait to tell Dawn the news. We continued packing for our trip. We were looking forward to our vacation.

A few days later we arrived at our destination in Canada. We called home to Dawn's mom. She told us that Wayne's brother Carl had called to inform her that Wayne had passed away the day after I visited him in the hospital. He also said that they would hold up the funeral until I returned. I knew most of our vacation was ahead of us.

I called Waynes's family and encouraged them to go ahead with the funeral service. The important thing was that I had been with him a day before we left and had the wonderful opportunity to pray with him to accept Jesus as his Savior. I didn't want people at Wayne's funeral to honor me, instead of giving Jesus all the honor He so greatly deserved.

Many folks had been involved in leading Wayne Kruen to the Lord -- his family, the church, Christian school teachers, friends, high school classmates, and a host of others. Some had planted the seeds, many watered and cultivated the seeds that began growing years before, and in this case, God chose me to come in for the harvest. I was humbled and reminded of 2 Corinthians 5:20, "We are therefore Christ's Ambassadors, as though God were making his appeal through us. We implore you on Christ's behalf: Be reconciled to God." [NIV] Wow! God was using me and I was **maturing** as an Ambassador of Jesus.

***

There was a time in my life when I dreamed that my political career would reach a pinnacle by receiving a presidential appointment as a United States Ambassador to a foreign country. I prayed about it and knew that if it happened it would be a miracle from God, and I knew that was possible.

Toward the end of my time working in Eastern Europe, I thought the day was coming. A special friend of mine who was an MP (Member of Parliament) in Romania told me that in a couple of days, he and the President of Romania planned to fly to the United States for a visit with President George W. Bush. He shared that one of the items on their agenda was to suggest to President Bush that Mike Menning ought to be considered for his choice of U.S. Ambassador to Romania. I had not asked them, I knew that was not the way it was usually done, but I was excited. Well, you guessed it, I did not receive the invitation to serve as the U.S. Ambassador to Romania.

Later in my life, as I prayed about this, the Lord made it clear in my heart that my ambassadorship had *already* been issued. I wanted to be an Ambassador for the President of the United States, but God granted me an Ambassadorship of the King of the Universe, for Jesus the Son of God, the Creator of the Universe. That ambassadorship was far greater than being the ambassadorship representing the President of the United States. God is so good!

"We are therefore Christ's ambassadors, as though God were making his appeal through us." 2 Corinthians 5:20a [NIV]

Reflections & Pondering

Section 5

Chapters 13-15

So we are Christ's ambassadors; God is making his appeal
through us. We speak for Christ when we plead,
"Come back to God."
2 Corinthians 5:20 [NLT]

Reflections on Your Life

"Don't Take Your Guns To Town" is a riveting story. It deals with the seriousness of working in such a mission field, it brings forward serious questions, and it is somewhat hilarious in the end. What are some of the serious questions it conjures up? What is your takeaway from the story in light of Psalm 44:6-7?

As you reflect on "Old Orange," it is obvious Mike likes to have fun in his storytelling but also brings to your attention possible dangers and risks when doing ministry. Did you have any other takeaways from the "Old Orange" story?

In the first book of the trilogy, Mike talks about angels appearing in his life and in the lives of a couple of others. In chapter 14, he tells of the appearance of angels at his brother Johnnie's hospital window, the angel of good news in the governor's race, and the two angels as he passed security guards on his way to the office of the CEO of Intermountain Healthcare. Then he tells the stories of Don Piper,

Marvin Besteman, and Charles Spurgeon's death where angels were present. As you reflect on these stories, and a few passages such as Psalm 91:11-12, Hebrews 1:14, and Hebrews 13:1-2, what is your response? Do you agree that angels appear to people today? Do you remember God sending angels your way?

What are your thoughts concerning parts of the books of Marv Besteman and Don Piper?

The role of an ambassador of the United States to another country is to represent the President of the United States as its highest-ranking diplomat in carrying out the President's foreign policy in that country. The job description of an ambassador of Christ is "We are therefore Christ's ambassadors, as though God were making his appeal through us." 2 Corinthians 5:20a. How would you compare the two "ambassadorships"?

As you reflect on the stories of Mike's witnessing to others in this section and the words of Matthew 28:19-20, The Great Commission, are you now more enthused about witnessing to others and leading them to Christ? What do you plan to do with what God has now put on your heart?

Do you have other questions or further comments about the stories in Chapters 13, 14, or 15?

Pondering <u>Your</u> Life's Direction

What are the **Life Changes** you need to make before you accept Jesus' offer of ambassadorship if you have not already done so?

Section Six
Life Beyond Imagination

Sixteen
Life Beyond Imagination

*...Now set your sights on the rich treasures and joys of heaven
where he sits beside God in the place of honor and power.
Let heaven fill your thoughts; don't spend your time
worrying about things down here.*
Colossians 3:2-3 [TLB]

*But there's far more to life for us. We're citizens of high heaven!
We're waiting for the arrival of the Savior, the Master, Jesus Christ,
who will transform our earthly bodies into glorious bodies
like his own. He'll make us beautiful and whole with the same
powerful skill by which he is putting everything as it
should be, under and around him.*
Philippians 3:20-21 [The Message]

I am reminded of God's incredible love for our family as I have been sharing my life memories. As I look back at the sunrise and the midday of my life, I see how God has used me to carry out His plans. I now look toward the sunset and I am seeing something different, a second sunrise of my life!

Once T.S. Elliot said, "The end of life is just the beginning," and I totally agree! The Colossians passage above leads me in my thinking and understanding that the sunset is ahead, but just beyond the sundown there is another sunrise, even more magnificent and glorious than anything familiar to mankind. I see the greatest, most exciting part of my life lying ahead. It is the part of my life so beautifully described in Revelation 21:1-4. "I saw Heaven and earth new-created. Gone the first Heaven, gone the first earth, gone the sea. I saw Holy Jerusalem, newly-created, descending resplendent out of Heaven, as ready for God as a bride for her husband. I heard a voice thunder from the Throne: "Look! Look! God has moved into the neighborhood, making his home with men and women! They're his people, he's their God. He'll wipe every tear from their eyes. Death is gone for good— tears gone, crying gone, pain gone—all the first order of things gone." The Enthroned continued, "Look! I'm making everything new." [The Message]

As Joni Eareckson Tada says in her book, *Heaven, Your Real Home*, "The more homelike that heaven becomes the more you feel like a foreigner and exile on earth... But our citizenship is in heaven." Philippians 3:19-20 [NIV][1]

Based on my interpretation of the scripture here are some of my thoughts about life and death:

- I believe that my life, who I am, started at the moment of conception. I believe that one day death will come to my body if Christ hasn't returned while I am alive. Furthermore, I believe that the person I am, my soul, my personhood, will never experience death. My spirit will live forever, beyond the death of the tent in which I now live. My physical body, as I know it, will be raised from the grave when Jesus returns. My spiritual body, or in other words, my paradise body, will then be reunited with my resurrected body at the very moment that Jesus returns to this earth on the last day. To me, that is very, very exciting!!!!!

- When I consider other autobiographies, most authors begin

with their birth through the time they finish their books as they record stories of their lives.

- Some would say that by including this last chapter in my book, "Life Beyond Imagination," I am violating the standards of writing my autobiography because I am writing about events that have not happened. So, if you wish, consider this last chapter a novel. I go beyond the life of my earthly body since my body will die, but as for me, the real me – my spirit – will never miss a beat and I, the real me, will never die! I am excited to include my thoughts about what I *might* experience when I arrive in paradise. The Bible says I now see through a glass darkly. How can I use words to describe what heaven will be like? It can't be done. I can only reflect on what the scripture says about heaven, ponder it, and write reflections of my thoughts. I have also read extensively what others have written about what they have learned about heaven from their studies of scripture.

Joni Eareckson Tada, in the second edition of *Heaven - Your Real Home* says, "Heaven is too specific, too real, for language. If we've learned anything from the prophet Ezekiel and the apostle John, it's that heaven is real. It's not a state or a condition, but a place, a place with streets, gates, walls, and rivers. We are wrong in thinking that heaven is wispy, thin, and vaporous. It is the earth that is like withering grass, not heaven. What it takes to know the place that Jesus has gone ahead to prepare is faith. Faith is what God has to say about heaven from His Word. For when God chose to talk about heaven, He did so by using nouns and verbs, the syntax and grammar, of the Bible. And although He mainly expounded on heaven in highly symbolic books like Ezekiel and Revelation, these symbols are meant to be motivation for our minds and fodder for our faith."[2]

I have prayed that if it pleases my Abba, Daddy, my journey to heaven will be the greatest trip of my life – you noticed I didn't say death. I pray that as I ascend from the surface of the earth I will be able to see and experience just a small part of God's indescribable creation.

At this point, I can only think of all this in human terms. But, as Eugene Peterson says in his translation of 1 Corinthians 13:12, "We don't yet see things clearly. We're squinting in a fog, peering through a mist. But it won't be long before the weather clears and the sun shines bright! We'll see it all then, see it all as clearly as God sees us, knowing Him directly just as he knows us!" [The Message]

I certainly don't know how God is going to answer my prayer, but I believe that when I am in paradise, God could allow me to see his great creation, far beyond the earth and this galaxy. If He allows me to see this on my trip home, I will be grateful, and if He doesn't, I will be just as pleased because God is perfect. He's God, and I'm not!

The story is told of Tim Keller, perhaps one of the most highly esteemed conservative theologians of the 21st century, receiving an incredible peace from God just before major surgery. He saw the massive universe and in that scene, there was one dark speck. Then he realized that the dark speck was the earth. He told of how God loved the creation of the earth and his people on the earth. He went on to say that after seeing the love of God for His people, he received the peace of going to heaven and being with God for all eternity.

I wonder … I can only imagine … I believe with all my heart that God will not keep the great universe that He has created all to himself. I think there is a real possibility that God will allow humans to see and experience more of his creation when we go to paradise that He has created for us. Jesus said I am going to prepare a place for you. Wow, at times I find it hard to wait, but I know that God has already decided the exact time for me to leave this earth and it will be at just the right time.

John R. Cross in his book, *The Stranger on the Road to Emmaus*, published by Goodspeed International, tells us that God is the great Creator and tells of the awesomeness of God!

Consider this, at the speed of light, which is created by God, we can begin to imagine just a flicker of knowledge about the size of the universe. Cross says that one can "circle the earth seven times at the speed of light in one second... pass by the moon in two seconds... Mars in four minutes, and Pluto in five hours."[3] Wow, in human measurements, traveling at the speed of light, I could reach the nearest star in a little over four years.

Traveling with my angelic escort, if God allows me to do that, and moving at the speed of light, I could cross the gigantic Milky Way Galaxy, from one end to the other, in an estimated 100,000 human years. Some scientists estimate that there could be 100 billion galaxies. We know that we serve a marvelous God!

I can't get my mind around these figures and measurements. God is awesome and words can't begin to describe the awesomeness of the creation. How can I describe what paradise or heaven will be like? Through scripture, God has opened a tiny crack in the door to heaven, so we can ponder its reality.

Oh, God, I will be thrilled with whatever way You choose for my journey home. I know it will be the right one. Who knows, maybe I will be taken home like the thief on the cross when Jesus said, "Today you will be with me in paradise." Oh, by the way, I am looking forward to meeting that guy when I arrive!

I don't know what the journey will be like. I also don't know where paradise is. No one knows because God chose not to tell us. Maybe it is beyond the universe which I have just tried to describe. Maybe it is in another realm. Maybe it's all around us and we can't see it.

Perhaps, I could be escorted there by angels. Luke 16:22 says, "The poor man died and was carried by the angels to Abraham's side." [ESV] I like to think that I will be able to embrace those angel escorts, just imagine, they might very well be the same angels who protected me while on earth.

I expect to see the most glorious light imaginable in heaven. Revelation 22:5 "And night will be no more; they will need no light of lamp or sun, for the Lord God will be their light, and they will reign forever and ever." [ESV]

God has given me many years on earth, and as several of my Biblical heroes have said, I am old and full of years. God has guided me on my earthly journey through times of significant challenges, sadness, joy, fulfillment, and excitement.

One disappointment in my life is that God hasn't allowed us to see the healing of Michael's brain injury. We accept it, but struggle with it. As Jesus prayed in the Garden of Gethsemane, "... nevertheless, not as I will, but as you will." Matthew 26:39 [ESV]

I praise God that Michael has learned to say a few words including, "Mom, Pa, and Ike" – his word for Mitch. He can combine the "m" from mom and "ike" and then say his name "Mmmike." He also can say, "bye." He makes attempts at certain sounds for a few other words. Through his made-up signs and sounds, we communicate and understand him, at least most of the time, and for that we praise God!

Michael has an incredible love for music and has praised God in his music! I sometimes joke that we always need to be nice to Michael because he could lead us as our heavenly choir director. We know that one day when Michael is called home, he will be fully healed – perfect. I like to imagine what it will be like to see Michael in heaven, healed – I can only imagine!

In my mind's eye, I can only imagine my angelic escort arriving at a most unexpected time. On my way to my heavenly home, I see a glow unlike any I have ever seen. Suddenly, I am in the midst of a place that at first glance reminds me of a Thomas Kinkade painting. However, it is thousands of times more lush and beautiful than any earthly painting. Oh, the beauty is beyond what I ever dreamed possible! The lush grass, flowers, trees, flowing brooks, the River of

Life, the animals, the sea creatures, and alas, the people. As it says in Luke 19:40, "if these were silent, the very stones would cry out." [ESV] The people are as warm and loving as a mother holding her newborn baby.

I see Jesus, the Son of God, the Jesus of the Bible, the Supreme Creator of all things. He is the one I have known and loved for so many years. I feel peace, love, and joy as never before. His face exudes love and His voice sounds like nothing I have ever heard. I recognize the Shepherd's voice. Jesus smiles, I see it as the warmest and most inviting smile; no earthly words can describe what I am experiencing. Jesus calls my name, *Marion, welcome home, good and faithful servant, thanks for working so hard to accomplish the purpose in life for which I created you!*

I'm home at last. I drop to my knees and worship my Lord and Savior. I don't know how long I stay on my knees; it seems like a long time and, yet, strangely, like a short time. I feel His gentle hands on my shoulders and then He lifts my face to meet His. Jesus holds out His nail-scarred hand, I know the nails were driven through His hands and feet for me. With joy and admiration, I worship Him, the King of Kings, and Lord of Lords. He takes my hand in His, I stand and behold the majesty and glory!

The great Creator of the Universe embraces me with a gentle, firm hug, more tender than anything I have ever felt! Together, we walk. I am in the beauty and holiness of my Savior. We spend time together and then he says, *Enjoy being with your new family, your brothers and sisters. You know our eternal family is coming together. There is something very special ahead for you. I will be with you whenever you want.*

"Before you leave, I have a question, Lord."

"Yes, I know," Jesus answers, *"it's about Michael. Oh, he was warmly welcomed and admired when he arrived. He is now whole, he is healed, he is a lead singer here in paradise – he sings a lot. Of*

course, everyone loves him, here everyone loves everyone."

Jesus goes on to tell me that Michael carries with him some of the same likable and peaceful characteristics we saw in him while on earth.

I am surrounded by many people; one by one, they embrace me.

I remember the words of 1 Corinthians 3:6, "I planted the seed, Apollos watered, but God gave the growth." [ESV] I gave my testimony, preached in many churches and other gatherings, and explained the way of salvation. I prepared the soil, planted the seeds, cultivated the new plants, and in some cases, God gave me the privilege of coming in for the harvest. Some of those seeds fell on good soil, they sprouted, they grew, and now they are here in heaven! Here in heaven, I meet people who heard me speak the Gospel and received Christ. I built on the work of others and others built on the work I was called to. I look forward to meeting others who planted and those who watered the seeds. On earth I only saw the back side of the tapestry, now I see the beauty of the tapestry, the finished story.

I see Bill, Wayne, Wendell, the lady on the road construction site, the scam caller guy from Nigeria, the woman in the airplane on the flight to Minneapolis, Jim, Luke, Lon, Tony, Janice, Bryanna, Carol, Chris, Jim, Jo, Larry, Will, Walter, and people from the polygamist community.

I see Rev. Peter DeBoer walking toward me. He was the only pastor I knew until I was fifteen years old. He taught me how to accept Jesus into my heart when I was just six years old. We had wonderful times together.

I am welcomed home by family members who have gone before me. I see my parents, Dawn's parents, and many other relatives from my days on earth. The reunion is precious and indescribable.

I meet thousands of people — family members going back many generations – who believed in Jesus before me. There are millions more and my love for them swells.

I see many of the Bible characters who arrived thousands of years before me. One of the people I always wanted to meet is coming in my direction and I know who he is - the thief on the cross who hung next to Jesus. He has a friendly smile and it is like we are old friends who haven't seen each other for a long time. We embrace and it seems as though my spiritual body and his merge for a few seconds. He defended Jesus and believed Him to be the Son of God. He was told by Jesus as they both hung on the cross, "Today, you will be with me in paradise." And here he is, greeting me in paradise!

I see people from every tribe, every nation, every color, and every age. I could never have imagined such beauty. I see small children and babies, filled with joy, worshiping and praising God.

They welcome me home. While on earth, I tried to serve my Lord with all my heart, and I am now receiving my rewards. I am in my new, spiritual body. Back in my hometown of Edgerton, Minnesota, my body, the tent in which I lived while on earth, was gently and lovingly lowered into the grave at the Hillside Cemetery in a few days. My spiritual body looks very similar to my earthly body, but now it is perfect.

I am reminded of 2 Corinthians 5:1, " For we know that if the tent that is our earthly home is destroyed, we have a building from God, a house not made with hands, eternal in the heavens." [ESV]

I know that one day when Jesus returns to the earth I will come straight up from that grave, just four miles south of where I was born early on July 27, 1945. Like Jesus, I will be raised from the dead, and united with my new earthly body. But, until that great and glorious day, I am blessed with this new spiritual body.

As I walk farther into paradise, I find myself in one of the most beautiful scenes I have ever seen. I see babies being loved and cared for. There are thousands, millions of babies and young children.

I have many questions to ask Jesus, and there He is, right beside me. I ask Him about all the babies and young children communicating

182

total joy and happiness, a sight beyond description, with loving caregivers numbering in the thousands. With excitement in His voice, Jesus tells me that many of the babies were stillborn, some babies were the result of miscarriages, some died as infants, and many who had been aborted. Also, as reported in the Old Testament, countless children had been offered to the false gods such as Molech, and were now in heaven.

Some parents later regretted their choice to end their child's life. Many of the mothers and fathers asked for forgiveness for this great sin and some accepted Jesus as their personal Savior and are now serving children. Jesus tells me that some of the brothers and sisters I see as caregivers were doctors and nurses who performed abortions. *"For all those who asked for forgiveness,"* Jesus said, *"I forgave them. Upon their arrival in heaven, some of these people requested to provide care for the babies and the children."*

Other caregivers are people who grieved on earth about the fact that they were never able to conceive children. Upon arrival in heaven, some have the opportunity to care for children who died young. Jesus says, *"This is one of their great rewards."*

So many thoughts rush through my mind, but I realize, there is no hurry because I have all the time I desire in heaven to process each thought. I remember the words Jesus comforted us with a few days before he left the earth. "In my Father's house are many mansions; if it were not so, I would have told you. I am going to prepare a place for you. And if I go and prepare a place for you, I will come again and receive you to Myself; that where I am, there you may be also. And where I go you know, and the way you know." John 14:2-4 [NKJV]

Jesus went to prepare a place for me and I am in that "place." Paradise is only the first stop for my new eternal life. Next, there will be the New Heaven and New Earth.

I hear a voice calling my name; it is the Apostle John. "I've been told how you loved what I wrote about in Revelation 21:1-4,

"Then I saw a new heaven and a new earth; for the first heaven and the first earth had passed away, and the sea was no more. I also saw the Holy City, the new Jerusalem, coming down out of heaven from God, prepared like a bride adorned for her husband. Then I heard a loud voice from the throne. Look, God's dwelling is with humanity, and he will live with them. They will be his people, and God himself will be with them and will be their God. He will wipe away every tear from their eyes. Death will be no more; grief, crying, and pain will be no more because the previous things have passed away." [ESV]

I thought back to reading this passage when I was on earth. I see what the apostle meant by describing what he saw in that new heaven. Everything around me is more gorgeous than earthly words can describe. I see what he meant in the last part of the verse when he wrote, "and the sea was no more." When I was on earth this little passage greatly troubled me, I hardly dared to talk about it! I mean it was scary to think about a new heaven and new earth without the ocean, no sandy beaches, no surfs, no crashing of waves, I wondered about it.

Scholars believe that in the day of the Apostle John, the sea was considered a place of the beast, where evil was resting and might come out to attack man. But, now I see the ocean and the sea teaming with life, a perfect place, an intimate part of all creation. The sounds of the sea are praising God as I never imagined!

Romans 8 records how creation will be affected on that great day when Jesus returns, mankind and creation will be released from the power of sin! Yes, creation will leap for joy. Maybe even rocks will cry out with praise for the Savior, as described in God's Word.

I see another man coming near. I am amazed that I know him also, although he is different from what I had envisioned while on earth. I am face-to-face with Isaiah, the great prophet and writer of one of the books of the Old Testament. He is loved by so many on earth. His greeting is a warm smile and a hardy welcome. The embrace is wonderful, for we have spiritual bodies. Isaiah quoted to me from the book he wrote recorded in chapter 11, translated by Eugene Peterson in "The Message:"

"The wolf will romp with the lamb, the leopard sleeps with the kid. Calf and lion will eat from the same trough, and a little child will tend them. Cow and bear will graze in the same pasture, their calves and cubs grow up together, and the lion eats straw like the ox. The nursing child will crawl over rattlesnake dens, the toddler sticks his hand down the hole of a serpent. Neither animal nor human will hurt or kill on my holy mountain. The whole earth will be brimming with knowing God-Alive, a living knowledge of God ocean-deep, ocean-wide."

Isaiah told me that when these words were put in his heart, God was referring to the New Heaven and New Earth. He said, "This will come after Christ returns to the earth for the final judgment." We talked as we walked along through a meadow. I was concerned that I was stepping on some of the flowers, but Isaiah laughed a little and said, "Don't worry about it. We're not on earth. There's no death here, and you can't kill or damage the flowers, even if you step on them." I looked back to where I had walked, the flowers I had stepped on sprang up immediately and looked as beautiful as before.

There is no hurry and I am relaxed and energized beyond explanation. No one here has a concern about time, because time is no longer, there is only the incredible joy of the day. I have a wonderful feeling of peace when suddenly Jesus is standing beside me, his hand on my shoulder, *"Come, I want you to meet more of* **our** *family."* Before I could only imagine, yet now here He is! I am in awe; I am talking with my Savior, the great Creator, my Lord, the Triune God - yes, he is my brother!

We are no longer in the meadow. I hear singing in the distance, it gets louder and louder and more and more glorious.

I am reminded of a time when I was a state senator and was asked to speak at a gathering of a charismatic Catholic group in Minneapolis called "The Servants of the Lord." I thought I would be speaking at a small Bible study of about a dozen people in a room at the DeLaSalle High School. When we arrived, much to my surprise, my host took me to a large auditorium filled with about two thousand people. This was something I had not experienced previously before in my life or ever again. I fully sensed the powerful presence of the Holy Spirit. As I spoke I felt His Spirit working in me. The evening concluded with a time of praise and worship. The great host of people was singing in tongues. I felt like I was being swept away into glory. I knew that what I experienced that night at that high school auditorium had been a small glimpse of heaven.

Here in heaven, countless people are worshiping. I can see the throne of God and know it is He seated on the throne, the great God and Father of the Universe. People and angels are singing, worshiping, and praising God, it seems as if they are without number, far greater than the sands of the seashores or the stars of the sky. Cherubim are flying back and forth singing and shouting praise to God forever and ever!

The worshippers are together, and yet some are separated into groups. I catch a glimpse of one particular group and it seems like they are more from my era.

From a distance I see the lead singer. He is a handsome young man. There is something unusual, beautiful, and familiar about him. Though I am a considerable distance from him, his crystal clear tenor voice has a fullness and grandeur like nothing I heard on earth. It is heavenly and sounds familiar. As I draw closer to the magnificent sound, I look at my Shepherd and see that His face is glowing with excited anticipation, knowing something great is about to happen. The singing is drawing to a close. The praise is paused. That young man leaves his position in the choir and is running toward me. Now I see it! Michael, my son, my dear son Michael who I always loved in ways

186

words cannot describe.

I begin to shout, praising Jesus, "Thank you! I praise you!" Michael cries out in joy, "Pa, Pa!" Michael is speaking in a clear voice that I hear for the first time. His brain injury is no longer! He hugs me, the greatest embrace, beyond any earthly embrace, and my heart is joyful beyond imagination. Michael tells me how thankful he is that I am here. His brain is fully healed, his body is healed, everything about him is perfect, and he looks majestic.

Together, Jesus, Michael, and I hug each other tightly. We are healed and perfect. Now we, and all who had gone before me, are a new family with greater love than was ever experienced by anyone while on earth. The rest of those who have been chosen by God and have accepted His offer have not yet arrived.

I am praising God that all the King's ambassadors are welcome to be forever with our Triune God and all the heavenly hosts. Part of my new family is together for all eternity, I am waiting for others to arrive.

I am home at last.

Reflections & Pondering
... we are Christ's Ambassadors

Section 6
Chapters 16

*So we are Christ's ambassadors; God is making his appeal
through us. We speak for Christ when we plead,
"Come back to God."*
2 Corinthians 5:20 [NLT]

Reflections on <u>Your</u> Life

Mike is not shy about telling the world that he thinks much about
looking past the sunset of his life into what he calls the second sunrise
of his life. He talks of heaven as his real home and that his citizenship
is not here, as expressed in Philippians 3:20, "But we are citizens of
heaven, where the Lord Jesus Christ lives!" [NLT] Do you live as
though you are a citizen of Heaven?

A popular saying a few years back and even today is, "Some people
are so heavenly-minded that they are no earthly good." Do you have
any thoughts or comments about that phrase in light of Philippians
3:20?

**In light of the scripture can you give answers about heaven to the
following questions?**

When you get to heaven do you think you will recognize believers
who went before you? Why?

Who do you think might greet you upon your arrival?

Who are some of the Bible characters you are looking forward to meeting upon your arrival?

What are your thoughts concerning Mike and Dawn's prayer asking God that their son, Michael, be taken to Heaven before they pass?

Jesus said, "In My Father's house are many mansions; if it were not so, I would have told you. I go to prepare a place for you." John 14:2 [NKJV] Do you dream of your "mansion," or a new place in that new heaven and new earth? What are your thoughts?

Do you have other thoughts about "beyond the sunset of your life"?

Pondering <u>Your</u> Life's Direction

Do you have other questions or further comments about this chapter, **Life Beyond Imagination?**

Are you experiencing **HEAD** and/or **Heart Changes** as you read the last chapter of **Ambassadors of Jesus?**

Author's note

One of the reasons I wrote the trilogy with the theme of **Ambassadors of Jesus** was because God placed in my heart the need to take God's command seriously as recorded in 2 Corinthians 5:20. We must tell future generations of His faithfulness in our lives. I pray that you will examine your life, make the changes that need to be made, and ask God to show how *you* are to tell of God's faithfulness to future generations.

For those of you who have read **Maturing as Ambassadors of Jesus** and have not yet accepted Christ as your personal Savior, you too can have peace in your heart, by giving your life to Jesus for all eternity, instead of being lost in the eternal separation from God. "For God so loved the world that He gave His one and only son, that whoever believes in him, shall not perish but have eternal life." [NIV] John 3:16

I encourage you to find a quiet place with the Bible in your hand and come before God. Ask him to give you an understanding of the following scriptures. I have shared these verses with many people as

I led them to a saving knowledge of Jesus Christ, He desires that all people come to Him.

Understanding these words could be the most important thing you have ever done. (Note, all eight passages in the NIV translation)

- Romans 3:23 - "**for all have sinned and fall short of the glory of God.**"
- Romans 6:23 - "For the wages of sin is death; but the **free gift** of God is eternal life in Christ Jesus our Lord."
- John 3:3 - Jesus replied, "Very truly I tell you, no one can see the kingdom of God **unless they are born again.**"
- John 14:6 - Jesus answered, "I am the way and the truth and the life. No one comes to the Father except **through me.**"
- Ephesians 2:8-9 - "For it is **by grace** you have been saved, through faith—and this is not from yourselves, it is the gift of God – not by works, so that no one can boast."
- 2 Corinthians 5:15 - "**And he died for all**, that those who live should no longer live for themselves but for him who died for them and was raised again."
- Romans 10:9-10 - "If you declare with your mouth, "Jesus is Lord," and **believe** in your heart that God raised him from the dead, you will be saved. For it is with your heart that you believe and are justified, and it is with your mouth that you profess your faith and are saved."
- Revelations 3:20 - "**Here I am!** I stand at the door and knock. If anyone hears my voice and opens the door, I will come in and eat with that person, and they with me."

If you have not already accepted Jesus as your personal Savior, I believe God is asking you to respond today. He has been patient with you, but today He is standing at the door of your heart. He is knocking, and the door has a door knob on only one side, your side of the door. God doesn't force His way in, He simply knocks. The Holy Spirit is asking you to open the door. It's up to you to repent of your sins and invite Him to come into your heart. If you invite Him in and give your life to Him, He will give you eternal salvation. This is the reason Jesus came to earth: to suffer and give his life as the sacrifice for your sins and mine.

If after reading **Maturing as Ambassadors of Jesus**, you would like to talk with me about your decision to ask Jesus into your heart -- or just wish to talk with me -- I would be pleased to hear from you. You can contact me through my website www.mikemenning.com or you can call me at (801) 915-3201.

If I don't meet you on this life's journey, I look forward to getting to know you. I look forward to being with you, with all who have ever believed, and with our Triune God in heaven for all eternity!

Be encouraged and use your life to become an Ambassador of Jesus! I am looking forward to meeting you on the other side.

Acknowledgments

My greatest acknowledgment goes to God for my life's journey. I pray that through God's leading, Part Two of the Trilogy, *Maturing as Ambassadors of Jesus* will encourage you to seek a closer walk with Him!

I give much credit and thanks to my wife Dawn as she patiently, chapter by chapter, edited my writing. Believe me, due to my Dutch, story-telling heritage, I often mix up prepositions, both in speaking and writing, by "throwing the cow over the fence some hay." Now I realize that I should have taken high school and college English and writing classes more seriously.

For several years, Dawn put up with me taking many of my spare minutes to write these books. One evening in November 2020, I closed my laptop, stood up from the couch, and said, "It is finished." I realized that I had about 40% more work to do in editing, proofreading, and getting *Ambassadors of Jesus* published. Time moved on and Dawn patiently responded to the many, many times when I was working on details and would say, "I am having a computer challenge, this paragraph has suddenly appeared on the 90 pages. Oh, rats, I think I just lost 20 pages! I don't know what's going on with this computer." She would drop what she was doing and come over to help me. Dawn was truly my tutor and I.T. person. I am grateful for her being at my side for these last 55-plus years of marriage.

A huge thanks to our son, Mitch, for helping me with the many technical challenges in getting the first manuscript *Boppa's Journey* into print for my grandkids. He worked on formatting, placing each chapter into one document, and did another edit of the first manuscript. Mitch got the original manuscript printed into book form and I gave *Boppa's Journey* to our grandchildren and a few others for Christmas 2020.

Our computer crashed just before the final draft during COVID. As we tried to take the material off the hard drive more problems arose. Many people tried to help. Then Matt Johnson said he thought he knew how to fix the problem and he did. That glitch set us back by about six months. Matt, thanks for coming to the rescue.

A big thanks to my niece Sheri Rodriguez who believed in Uncle Marion's first manuscript and showed it to her friend Lorilee Cracker, a professional editor. That got the ball rolling on the idea of publishing the trilogy.

Lorilee Cracker served as one of my professional editors. She was patient with me while she saved the very heart of the message. She took out over 20,000 words from my original manuscript! Lorilee, it's been an honor to become "Uncle Marion" to you.

Thanks to our friend Susie Nelson for sharing details of how she went about the publishing process of her book, *Failure of God.*

Jacqueline Croswhite did a yeoman's job in proofreading the third manuscript. She also made many suggestions on the chronology of events and suggested many clean-ups. Jacqueline, thanks.

Denise Buckley, God has given you a very bright mind and I

praise Him that you have shared your talents with me in proofreading the manuscript, for making many suggestions on the proper use of grammar, and for catching other very important details. Thanks for being part of the team.

I take my hat off to Crystal Drenth and Cobie Den Ouden, two sisters-in-law of mine who proofread this book. Thanks for your honesty and sharp eyes catching the use of too many commas and other glitches. Now you both know of my love affair with commas.

Sara Hobbs, I praise God for your patience in working with me, and for your God-given talents, wisdom, creativity, and energy you put into the work. Sara created the cover design, formatted the book, and helped us find our way through the jungle pathway of publishing a book. You were a real partner!

I also need to acknowledge a past friend, Chuck Colson, who arrived in heaven before me. Many years ago he physically twisted my arm while we were standing in the office of a mutual friend, Minnesota Governor Al Quie. He looked me in the eye and with all seriousness said to me, "Mike, you can do it. You can and should write a book about your son Michael and your life." Later, Chuck wrote the foreword in my first book, *Us Four, A Senator, His Family, Their Brain Injured Child.* Chuck, I love you and look forward to seeing you in heaven.

I was greatly impressed and moved when my brother-in-law Gaylin Den Ouden and his wife, Cobie, finished their books telling stories of their lives, to be given to their grandkids. That got me thinking that I needed to start telling the story of my life's journey.

Dawn's cousin Nelvin Vos challenged me many years ago. He suggested that I write down thoughts about our son Michael, our family, and how God took us through life. He said, "When you want to record it properly in a book you will have much of the material you need."

Thanks to my friend Steven Horton, who is the voice on the

Audible version of *Becoming Ambassadors of Jesus*. Steve, I appreciate the hundreds of hours and admire your God-given voice.

I am so grateful to the entire team of people who helped me along the way and encouraged me. Storytelling comes naturally to me, writing does not. Oh, don't get me wrong I enjoy writing, it is just using my fingers and the computer instead of my voice. But to turn the manuscript into the book takes a team of good, dedicated people; be it their encouragement along the way or the multitude of suggestions. Thanks, team.

Thanks to all who inspired this Minnesota farm kid along the way. I appreciate where I grew up and continue to see my roots as a farm kid from Edgerton. Sometimes I wonder if my heart has ever left the rural lifestyle, even as I serve as an ambassador of my Lord!

Notes

Foreword

1. Tada, Joni Eareckson, *A Spectacle of Glory: God's Light Shining through Me Every Day* (Zondervan, 2016). 338.

Introduction

1. Besteman, Marv with Lorilee Craker, *My Journey to Heaven* (Revell, 2012). 13.

Chapter 14: Angels Watching Over Me

1. Piper, Don, *90 Minutes in Heaven* (Revell, 2014). 38

Chapter 16: Life Beyond Imagination

1. Tada, Joni Eareckson, *Heaven: Your Real Home* (Zondervan Publishing House, 2018). 136-137 .

2. Tada, 40.

3. Cross, John P., *The Stranger on the Road to Emmaus* (Goodspeed International, 2001). 15-17.

More *Ambassadors of Jesus*

Did you enjoy reflecting and pondering your life's direction as you read *Maturing as Ambassadors of Jesus*? Read more of Marion's story and complete the *Ambassadors of Jesus* trilogy.

Book #1

Becoming Ambassadors of Jesus is an incredible story of God leading Mike Menning as a poor farm kid who experienced major depression, learned to read at age 25, went to college, was elected State Representative at age 29, and a State Senator at age 31. He and his wife faced life with their severely disabled son. It is Bible study and book club friendly. The reader will be riveted to the stories while laughing and crying.

Book #3

Michael, an Ambassador of Jesus is the all-telling reality of Michael's disability and the astounding progress of his damaged brain, the development through the extraordinary dedication of his parents working on a brain stimulation program ten hours a day, seven days a week, for most of four-and-a-half years. This book brings to light the Church's responsibility and attitude toward people with disabilities.

*Learn more or purchase book #1 and #3 at **mikemenning.com***

Made in the USA
Columbia, SC
16 April 2024

34465694R00133